Okoboji

Over 160 Years of History and Images

Hedgpeth Publishing, LLC

c/o Concierge Marketing

13518 L. Street

Omaha, NE 68137

Hardcover ISBN: 978-1-936840-57-1

Library of Congress Cataloging Number: 2016939332

Library of Congress Cataloging-in-Publication data on file with the publisher.

Photo credits

Front cover: The shoreline of Arnold's Amusement Park circa 1920. The building on the right was the pavilion that later became the Fun House. On the left was the Lakeside Department Store that in 1923 had a second story added to house the Roof Garden. Photos courtesy of the Iowa Great Lakes Maritime Museum (Arnold's Amusement Park circa 2014), Okoboji Tourism and Blue Water Ventures, David Thoreson.

Back cover: Sunset over West Lake Okoboji, September, 2015. Photo courtesy Jim Hedgpeth.

Title page: An early view of the grade, about 1900. Visible is the Smith Home on the bank, several tents and Wilson & Son's store. Photo courtesy of the Wilson family.

Printed in the USA

10 9 8 7 6 5 4 3 2 1

CONTENTS

PREFACE

I have spent time at Lake Okoboji since I was born. The Clarke family has been coming to the lake since the 1880s. Those who know me know I always have a "project" of some kind. In 2003 I co-wrote *The History and Memories of Des Moines Beach*. I was planning on expanding that book with an update, but that didn't happen. A neighbor suggested I write a history book about Okoboji. I thought about that for a couple of days and jumped into it.

Similar to the Des Moines Beach book, this has been a labor of love. My husband, Jim, would leave for work around 6:30 a.m. I would sit down at the computer shortly after his departure. He would find me there upon his return home. We would have dinner and talk about what I had discovered. He would then do the dishes while I was back working until about ten. I have never regretted any time spent on the book.

OKOBOJI: Over 160 Years of History and Images was a short-fuse book. Research began in early October 2015, with the goal of having it on the shelves by Memorial Day, 2016. This did provide a challenge going into winter with the majority of cottages being closed up. So many images were not available during this time. The Okoboji community was highly forthcoming, especially once they heard that my profits were going to the Okoboji Foundation.

With limited time to do the research, this book focuses on West Okoboji. However, to complete the story, I have included a few places not on West Lake.

The best part has been the incredible people I have talked to in researching the book. Jim and I were having lunch at the Okoboji Store and were sitting next to Donna Mau. Donna suggested I get in touch with Zeke Wilson's daughter, Doyne Wilson Hummel. (The Wilson family have long roots at the lake. They owned the businesses currently owned by the Mau family.) Doyne shared stories and let me borrow Zeke's scrapbooks. Fred Wilson's daughter, Loraine Wilson Little, provided wonderful photographs and stories as well.

I spent a lot of time at the Maritime Museum with Mary Kennedy. One day a gentleman came in, and I told him about the book and my research. That evening, Don McCulloch had me over to see what he had collected. Many images came from that serendipitous meeting.

The people at the Department of Natural Resources have been incredibly helpful. I learned so much through my many phone calls and meetings with Mike Hawkins. I loved my talks with Bill Maas, a former Lake Patrol officer. Neighbor Jane Shuttleworth, Lakeside Lab, walked over in the snow to bring me photographs and show me just how the lake would "flip" using colored ice.

It seemed as if every time I told someone about my project, he or she suggested someone new to talk to. I now have many new friends, like Fred Cerwick, who caught the image of the barge blowing up for the University of Okoboji homecoming fireworks display. He graciously touched up several images for the book as well as provided numerous photographs.

Thanks also to David Thoreson for allowing me to use several of his incredible photographs. They added so much to current-day Okoboji in this book.

Finally, this book would not be what it is without the guidance of Lisa Pelto and her team at Concierge Marketing, and my wonderful and insightful editor, Sandra Wendel.

I could go on and on. I apologize to those individuals I did not mention. You are no less important, and I thank you.

I hope visitors and generational local families discover new images and fun stories they were not aware of. I have tried to share the history, but also to give the reader a sense of what the lake is now. Next time you are caught inside on one of those rainy summer afternoons or chilly winter days, pick up this book and enjoy Okoboji as you've never seen before.

At work in Omaha…
and at Lake Okoboji.

INTRODUCTION

"I heard the National Geographic magazine proclaimed Okoboji to be one of the three 'true blue' lakes of the world."

→ *Read more in chapter seven.*

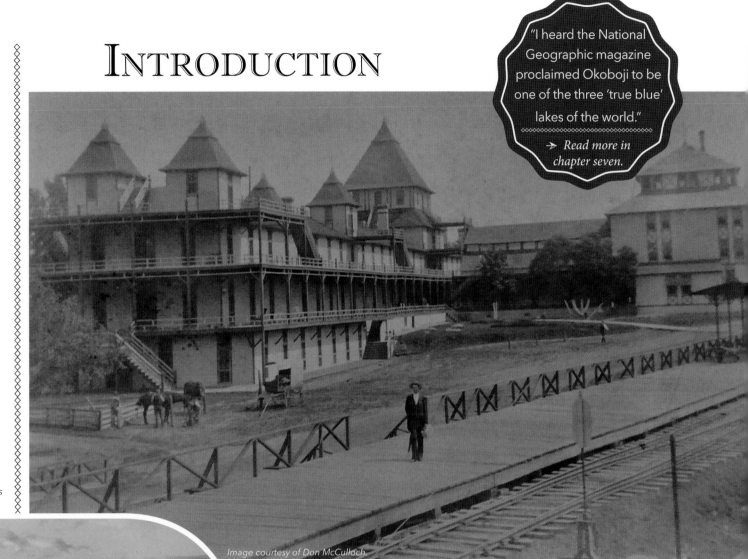

Image courtesy of the Iowa Great Lakes Maritime Museum.

Image courtesy of Don McCulloch.

"New York City is such a drag with Prohibition! We heard about a wonderful place in northern Iowa where the train drops you off at the most remarkable hotel and the liquor is flowing."

→ *Read more about these early revelers in chapter six.*

"Heard we are going to a place called Okoboozhy. Wherever is that, and whatever does that mean?"

→ *Find out in chapter eight.*

Scow Sailing on Okoboji   about 1910

Image courtesy of Martha Green.

Image courtesy of the Iowa Great Lakes Maritime Museum.

"That was in Okoboji?"

➔ *Find out just what it is and more in chapter seven.*

"Did you hear that the lake 'flips' twice a year! Will our boat turn over?"

➔ *Read about this natural phenomenon in chapter seven.*

AN OKOBOJI LANDMARK PROPERTY - FREDORA - HISTORICALLY ONE OF THE FINEST LOCATIONS ON WEST OKOBOJI

Unique! 88.5 ft. of West Okoboji Lakeshore with an incomparable full view of the lake. Faces southeasterly in to the prevailing summer breezes and is beautifully situated among the trees on a deep, heavily wooded lot. Location advantage of west shoreline of West Lake. Four bedrooms & full bath up and two bedrooms & full bath down. Two fireplaces and a 60' enclosed porch on lakeside. Large living room with brick fireplace, separate dining room, basement, partially furnished, and a 4 plank dock with sunning platform. Priced at little more than the lakeshore lot value! $295,000.

Image courtesy of Dickinson County Historical Society & Museum and Dickinson County News.

"Love the roaring twenties! We hit the road and headed to Lake Okoboji to buy a vacation cottage. Got a great one for $6,000."

➔ *Want to know the real estate history of lake lots? Find this information in chapter six.*

"So you mention the University of Okoboji."

➔ *For the real story, head to chapter six.*

Image courtesy of The Three Sons.

Image courtesy of the Iowa Great Lakes Maritime Museum.

Image courtesy of Iowa Great Lakes Maritime Museum.

"First a skating rink and a boat builder, then it included a post office, general store, boat livery, restaurant, fast food, then another restaurant! Where is this place?"

➜ *To see how this place changed so much since 1885, check out chapter three.*

"Who built the towering obelisk on the south side of West Lake Okoboji and why was the tragic event it honors so critical in lake history?"

➜ *Find out in chapter two.*

CASINO-TERRACE PARK, ON LAKE OKOBOJI, IOWA

"My husband and I love going to the Casino, but the kids especially love it! It is such a wholesome place for entertainment."

➜ *Where is this place called the Casino that doesn't have a roulette wheel? Check out chapter six.*

Image courtesy of the Iowa Great Lakes Maritime Museum.

IN THE BEGINNING

ack when vacationers first began to visit the various lakes that make up the Iowa Great Lakes region, Big Spirit Lake was considered the preferred lake. When you look at Big Spirit's statistics, it is understandable—with its 16.1 miles of shoreline and 5,367 acres of water. The banks are not steep and the beaches are plentiful. However, its average depth is only 17 feet with a maximum depth of 23 feet. At the end of the nineteenth century, it was thought to be going dry.

East Okoboji is more like a wide riverbed. It connects the spillway from Spirit Lake to the other lakes. East has 1,835 surface acres of water with 16.8 miles of shoreline. The average depth is only 10 feet with a maximum depth of 21 feet.

East connects with Upper Gar, a 37-acre lake, 1.4 miles of shoreline with an average depth of only 3.5 feet. From Upper Gar you reach Minnewashta, which has 126 surface acres of water, 2.3 miles of shoreline, an average depth of 10 feet and is 15 feet at its deepest point. The last lake of the chain is Lower Gar. It contains 254 acres of water, has 4 miles of shoreline, is 8.1 feet at its deepest with an average depth of 4 feet.

There is a plaque on the State Pier, written by Jean Prior (retired state geologist) that states:

> Fourteen thousand years ago the spot on which you are standing was covered under a mile-high ice sheet. The fourth Wisconsin glacier carved the cluster of lakes into northwest Iowa. While this north-south cut is typical of glacial lakes, West Okoboji is unusual because it is so deep.
>
> One theory is that a waterfall, coursing down the mile thick ice, gouged the lake bed to its depth of 136 feet or more. Or perhaps, the juggernaut of ice, shoving glacial rubble ahead of it, sculpted the 6.5 mile long basin to be filled by melting ice as the glacier retreated. Glacial deposits here are hundreds by hundreds of thousands of years the glacial deposit of most other Iowa landscapes.

The lakes were formed as part of the Bemis and Altamont moraine complexes of the Des Moines lobe of the Wisconsin glaciations. West Okoboji is an anomaly in this region.

Image courtesy of the Iowa Department of Natural Resources.

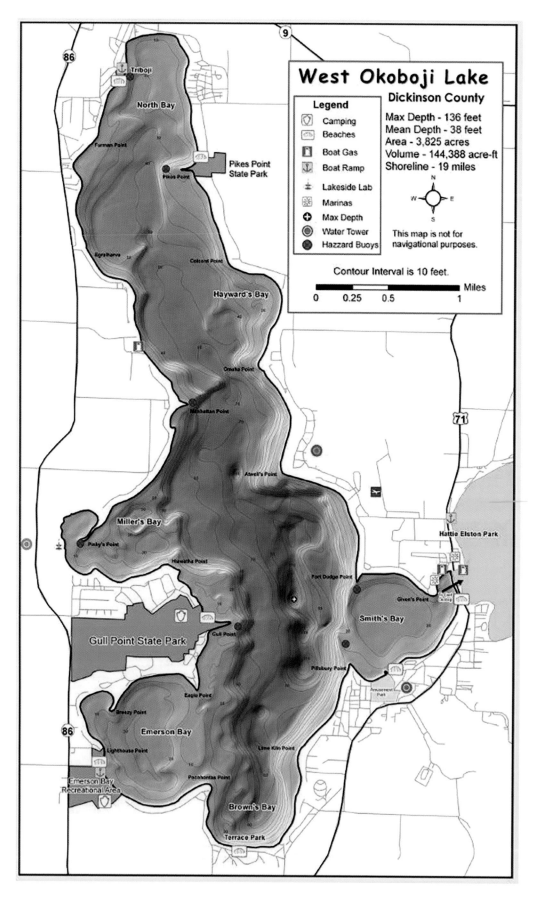

West Okoboji Lake
Dickinson County

Legend

- Camping
- Beaches
- Boat Gas
- Boat Ramp
- Lakeside Lab
- Marinas
- Max Depth
- Water Tower
- Hazzard Buoys

Max Depth - 136 feet
Mean Depth - 38 feet
Area - 3,825 acres
Volume - 144,388 acre-ft
Shoreline - 19 miles

This map is not for navigational purposes.

Contour Interval is 10 feet.

Miles
0   0.25   0.5   1

Mike Hawkins, Iowa Department of Natural Resources, explained there is no other natural lake with similar characteristics until you get to the northern half of Minnesota. In layman's terms, the thick slab of glacial ice moved back and forth where West Okoboji now is bounded. This was not a clear block of ice, but one with a lot of debris. There were most likely cracks and fissures through it, and the ice was thicker right in this location. Erosion from huge quantities of water melting from these massive ice sheets likely caused the incredible depth of West Lake Okoboji.

West Okoboji is a totally different body of water. Surrounding its 3,847 surface acres of water are many coves with somewhat steep banks. It has 19.8 miles of shoreline, but what makes the lake stand out is its depth. The average depth is 38 feet, but the maximum is 138 feet.

Image courtesy of the Iowa Department of Natural Resources.

2

THE MASSACRE

The lakes area was believed to be a sacred place to the Dakota Sioux Indians. The area was opened to settlers by a treaty signed in 1853 "giving" Iowa lands to white settlers and relocating the Indians to the Dakotas.

Sunday, March 8, 1857, started out as an icy cold day around the Iowa Great Lakes. The winter of 1856–1857 was the coldest on record. Snow was measured in feet.

Prior to that Sunday, Inkpaduta had been terrorizing settlers for weeks south of the lakes. He was in a foul mood as one of his companions had been killed to the south at Gillett Grove.

Just as the Gardner household was about to sit down to a meager Sunday breakfast, their door opened and a lone Indian came in. Soon, Inkpaduta and fourteen of his warriors, their squaws and children, were crammed in the cabin located west of the grade near the current amusement park on West Lake Okoboji. They took food and shortly after noon they left.

Everyone at the cabin was most disturbed by the attitude and behavior of the Indians. Two residents of the neighboring Granger cabin that had stopped in and witnessed Inkpaduta's behavior had left prior to the Indians' departure. They seemed unconcerned.

After leaving the Gardner cabin, the Indians headed northeast to the Mattock cabin. (This was just to the south of the isthmus between West and East lakes.) Midafternoon two men, Mr. Luce and Mr. Clark, took off from the Gardner cabin to check up on the residents of the Mattock cabin. About 3:00 p.m. shots were heard from the direction of the Mattock cabin.

Inkpaduta, a renegade Indian chief with his own tribe, was not part of the treaty meetings and did not agree with it. (Inkpaduta painting was painted in 1900 by nineteen-year-old Beth Allen Smith, Bruce Smith's grandmother.)

Image courtesy of Bruce and Vicky Smith.

MARBLE
2/1/1

SPIRIT LAKE

THATCHER
6/4/2

HOWE
8/8/0

GRANGER
4/4/0

WEST LAKE OKOBOJI

EAST LAKE OKOBOJI

MATTOCK
8/8/0

GARDNER
9/8/1

LABEL CODE: A/B/C
A - NO. PEOPLE IN CABIN AT THE TIME
B - NO. KILLED
C - NO. HELD CAPTIVE

Image courtesy of State of Iowa GIS and Leslie Suhr.

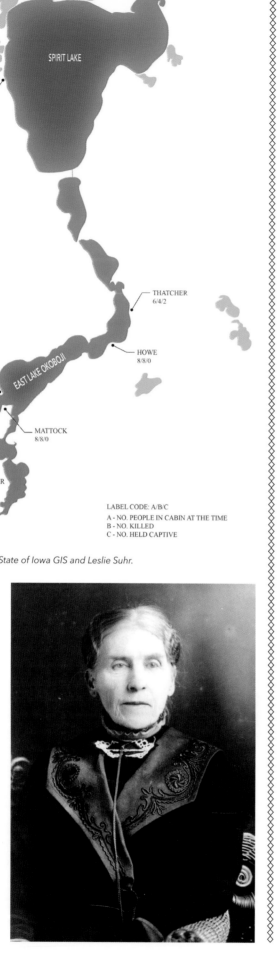

*Image courtesy of Iowa Great
Lakes Maritime Museum.*

As the sun was setting, Mr. Gardner stepped outside to see what was going on. He immediately returned to inform all, "Nine Indians are coming now only a short distance from the house and we are all doomed to die." His wife protested his use of any weapons and said, "If we have to die, let us die innocent of shedding blood."

The Indians entered the cabin, and as Mr. Gardner was reaching to give them more flour, he was shot in the back. The Indians then proceeded to kill all but young Abigail Gardner, whom they took prisoner. (It is from Abbie that most of the story is known.) That night they held a war dance outside the burning Mattock cabin. Four men from the nearby Granger cabin and eight people from the Mattock cabin were murdered there.

Monday morning, March 9, the Indians traveled across the ice heading northeast toward the Howe cabin, then to the Thatcher cabin. Everyone at those homes was killed with the exception of Mrs. Noble and Mrs. Thatcher. They were taken prisoner and joined thirteen-year-old Abbie at the Indians' camp.

Tuesday, March 10, everyone headed north, and on Wednesday, March 11, they arrived at Marble Grove (west side of Spirit Lake). They arrived at the Marble cabin, killed Mr. Marble and took Mrs. Marble hostage.

Thirty-one men, women, and children were killed at the lakes during those four days. Four women were taken hostage by Inkpaduta and his followers. Mrs. Thatcher and Mrs. Noble were killed on the march northwest. Mrs. Marble was sold and set free. Abbie Gardner was purchased by a band of Wahpeton Indians and soon set free.

> In 1891, after several years' absence, Abigail Gardner Sharp bought back her family's cabin. She restored it and charged admission to help pay bills. Abbie later moved to a cabin on Lake Minnewashta. She died in January 1921 in Colfax, Iowa. Mrs. Marble never returned to the lakes.

The initial discovery of the massacre was by a trapper named Morris Markham. He had actually stumbled into the Indian camp prior to their departure from the lakes area. He avoided them and brought the news to other trappers, two of whom traveled to Fort Dodge to report the incident. Markham traveled north and warned the settlers in the Jackson, Minnesota, area to beware.

At first, the stories of a massacre were not believed, but soon a burying party was assembled and headed north from Fort Dodge. They arrived after nine days of bitter travel. This was the coldest and snowiest season known. Many in the burying party perished. Others, including R.A. Smith, author of *The History of Dickinson County Iowa*, realized the incredible beauty of the land and lakes and decided to make their homes there.

The Gardner log cabin was sold by Abigail's son to the Iowa Conservation Commission in 1941. In 1974 it was transferred to the State Historical Society. During the 1975 restoration, the loft was removed to bring the cabin back to how it looked in 1856.

Image courtesy of Iowa Great Lakes Maritime Museum.

Image courtesy of Doyne Wilson Hummel and Dickinson County News.

The Gardner log cabin after the 1975 restoration.

Inkpaduta was never captured. He and two of his sons were present at the Battle of the Little Bighorn. It was one of his sons who killed Lieutenant Colonel George Armstrong Custer.

Abbie Gardner married Casville Sharp, a cousin of Elizabeth Thatcher, August 1857. They had three children. The Sharps separated, and Abbie moved back to the lakes. She made money speaking of her plight, and in 1885 wrote *History of the Spirit Lake Massacre and the Captivity of Miss Abbie Gardner*.

On July 26, 1895, a 55-foot tall granite obelisk was dedicated in honor of those who perished in the massacre. About 5,000 people attended the dedication at the cabin site. The state of Iowa provided $5,000 for the monument. It is constructed of rough and smooth Minnesota granite. The top is in the shape of an Indian arrow. Four bronze plaques, one on each side, tell the story.

Included on the grounds of the Gardner cabin are the obelisk monument, the pyramid stone shrine built by Abigail to honor her family lost in the massacre, graves, the cabin, and museum.

Image courtesy of Iowa Great Lakes Maritime Museum.

3

THE GRADE AND VICINITY

There is probably no better-known area at the lake, other than the amusement park, than "the grade." Most don't know it by that name. The grade is the narrow strip of land, in the town of Okoboji, that separates the east and west lakes.

Prior to the mid-1800s there was no bridge of any kind. This was an isthmus that could be crossed by swimming or wading about 30 feet from one side to the other.

The first bridge was a foot bridge of split logs. It was widened, and the county erected its first bridge in 1860. It was 210 feet long, split logs on trestles. There was a 30-foot span over the water.

In 1874 or 1875 the trestle was removed from the original foot bridge. The bridge now stood only four feet above the water. Soon there came the demand to travel between the lakes by a boat larger than just a rowboat. A block and tackle drawbridge was tried and failed miserably.

In 1883 three wonderful things happened at this location. First, the original swing bridge was built. Second was the construction of a large building by Louis Kellsen and S. E. Mills. Kellsen ran the upper level, which housed a roller skating rink. Mills ran a bait shop and rented out boats on the lower level. (This was called a livery.) The third and most influential occurrence was the arrival of railway service.

In 1887 W. S. (Bill) Wilson purchased the store property and business. He was from a farm near Sutherland and loved coming to the lakes to fish.

Painting by Amanda Smith Buckland, Milton Smith's (see pages 84-85) sister, showing the grading looking south toward Arnold's Park, 1876.

Image courtesy of Bruce and Vicky Smith.

Image courtesy of Loraine Wilson Little.

Fishing was great at the grade even back in the 1800s.

Mills Bros Boatmen building about 1885. The skating rink on the upper level was not a success and was converted to a general store and post office.

Image courtesy of Iowa Great Lakes Maritime Museum.

Image courtesy of Dickinson County Historical Society & Museum.

View looking south shows the early swing bridge and the low position of the first building at the grade.

Wilson & Sons ran the store and later the nearby Wilson Boat Works. The homes also belonged to the Wilson family.

Image courtesy of Loraine Wilson Little.

Mills store with steamboats *Illinois and Ben Lennox* at the landing.

Image courtesy of Doyne Wilson Hummel.

In 1915 Wilson & Sons sold the general store to Charlie Gipner. He ran it for a short while and sold it to Herman Wiese in 1919, who in turn sold it to Roy Smith and Mr. Elston in 1920. Zeke Wilson, son of Bill, fondly remembered when he would accompany Roy Smith around the lake taking grocery orders in the mornings and delivering them in the afternoons.

In 1920 Tom Olson purchased the Okoboji Store. Zeke helped in the livery. They were the first to rent boats with outboard motors.

When Zeke got older, he and his brother would help with the operation of the swing bridge. This went on from 1924 through 1929.

Image courtesy of Iowa Great Lakes Maritime Museum.

By 1898 the bridge needed to be "beefed up." It was rebuilt on concrete pilings. In 1909 a new steel bridge was erected. This was still a swing-style bridge to allow steamships like the *Iowa* to pass through.

Image courtesy of Doyne Wilson Hummel.

The swing bridge opened to let the *Des Moines* steamship pass from East to West Okoboji.

Image courtesy of Iowa Great Lakes Maritime Museum.

The old swing bridge was replaced with the first concrete bridge in 1929. (With the construction of roads encircling the lakes, there was no longer a need for the steamships to traverse from West to East Okoboji.) This was quite a project. The road was raised, as was the Okoboji Store to better align with the bridge and roadway. (The store was elevated 5 feet 8 inches!) There was also a restaurant and fish shop on the other side of the road (circa 1930).

Image courtesy of Luckybreak/Okoboji.

THE GRADE BRIDGE

TOM OLSON'S STORE+ BOAT LIVERY
OKOBOJI, IOWA D-284

Tom Olson's boat store and boat livery with the bridge and tunnel under the highway. The tunnel provided a way for neighboring residents to cross the busy highway and get to the post office and store.

Image courtesy of Luckybreak/Okoboji.

The Olson family ran the Okoboji Store from 1920 until selling it to Sylanious Nelson in 1943. It was sold in 1973 to Mrs. L. D. Colbert. The large Colbert family had a cottage on Des Moines Beach. Her sons ran a bakery in the back part of the store. (Their caramel rolls are still fondly remembered.)

Mrs. Colbert sold the building to James Miller in 1974. Sadly, the building was torn down on November 2, 1976. Miller built a new building on the site to house his franchise for Kentucky Fried Chicken.

The year 1976 was almost pivotal for the grade. The Iowa Department of Transportation was planning on widening the highway to four lanes. The entire Okoboji City Council boycotted the meeting on the advice of their attorney. (The state wanted to expand the two-lane road to four, which in this extremely narrow area would have been disastrous.) This project was stopped by an injunction, which was lifted in 1996 or 1997.

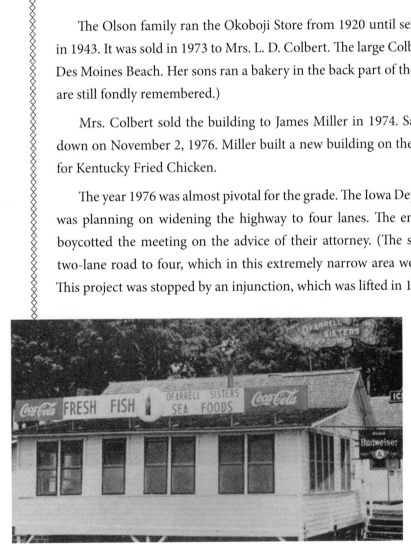

The O'Farrell Sisters Restaurant. In 1959, Newt Carson, the owner of the property, decided to raise their rent, so they moved up the hill.

Image courtesy of Iowa Great Lakes Maritime Museum.

The widening of Highway 71 began in 1998. The plan was no longer for a four-lane project, but was reduced to three lanes. The roadwork did mean the removal of the old Fisherman's Wharf restaurant. The current owner, Jerry Kirth, bought the KFC building from James Miller directly across the street and moved Fisherman's Wharf restaurant into it. Sadly, the old tunnel under the highway was removed. Happily, the town of Okoboji ended up with four stoplights, which is a blessing on busy summer weekends.

The building that housed Fisherman's Wharf also had quite a history. Ike Kissinger ran a restaurant there. The O'Farrell girls worked for him. In about 1947, Kissinger decided to run for Dickinson County Sheriff and didn't think he should own a restaurant/bar. The O'Farrell sisters took over the business.

Other businesses included an ice cream stand, Diver's Den, and Bay View Antiques. All the buildings located on the west side of the highway are long gone due to the widening of the highway.

The next restaurant at the site was named Mike's Fisherman's Wharf (circa 1960).

Image courtesy of O'Farrell family.

Image courtesy of Kenny Halibur.

In about 1963 Mike's became Harold's Fisherman's Wharf and was later owned by Jerry Kirth.

Okoboji Dairy
Ice Cream store,
owned by Byron
and Stella Smith.

Image courtesy of Peggy Smith Jones.

The grade in 2015. The highway is now three lanes wide with a stoplight at the far left of the photograph. There are no longer any businesses, or parking, on the west side of the highway.

Image courtesy of Mau Marine.

Diver's Den, 1969, owned by Rob Eves.

Image courtesy of Rob Eves.

The relocated Wharf restaurant was remodeled and renamed the Okoboji Store in 2015.

Image courtesy of Mau Marine.

4

ON THE MOVE

I n the late 1800s the main forms of transportation involved animals, wind, or steam. A covered wagon traveled ten to fifteen miles a day. A horse and carriage averaged four miles per hour.

The most significant addition that brought change to the Great Lakes area occurred in 1882 with the arrival of the railroad.

TRAINS

Early settlers urged several rail lines to come to the lakes. They knew a railroad would bring vacationers. However, before a line would be laid, the towns in the affected area would have to vote in an "aid" tax to help support the railroad. Time and time again, they believed a deal was set, right-of-ways established, but deals would fall through.

Finally in 1882, the lakes got their first train. The July 7, 1882, *Spirit Lake Beacon* announced the Burlington, Cedar Rapids & Northern Railway Company (a.k.a. Burlington) rails had reached the isthmus between Spirit Lake and East Okoboji.

The first train arrived July 11, 1882. The Burlington would end up having depots at Orleans, Spirit Lake, and West Okoboji by the mid-1890s. Their competitor was the Chicago, Milwaukee, St. Paul Railway (a.k.a. Milwaukee). This line reached the isthmus between West and East Okoboji on September 21, 1882.

Regular passenger service by the Milwaukee began on May 1, 1883. Service to Spirit Lake was established on September 18, 1883. The depots for this line included Arnold's Park, Okoboji, and Spirit Lake. Spirit Lake became the end point for the Milwaukee line. The train would drop off passengers, go to a roundabout about two blocks to the north, then head back south to Spencer and Des Moines.

The Burlington, Cedar Rapids & Northern Railway Company, later called the Chicago, Rock Island & Pacific, traveled from Chicago to Estherville, Orleans, Spirit Lake, West Okoboji, and on to Sioux Falls.

Image courtesy of Iowa Great Lakes Maritime Museum.

The first Hotel Orleans was built in 1883 by the Burlington, Cedar Rapids & Northern Railway Company. That tiny building at the end of the raised walkway was the depot. (The railroad wanted passengers to go to their hotel, not the depot.)

The West Okoboji depot and neighboring hotel were located at the north end of West Okoboji. The depot was moved and is now incorporated into the Northland Inn.

Image courtesy of Bob and Mary Ellen Evans.

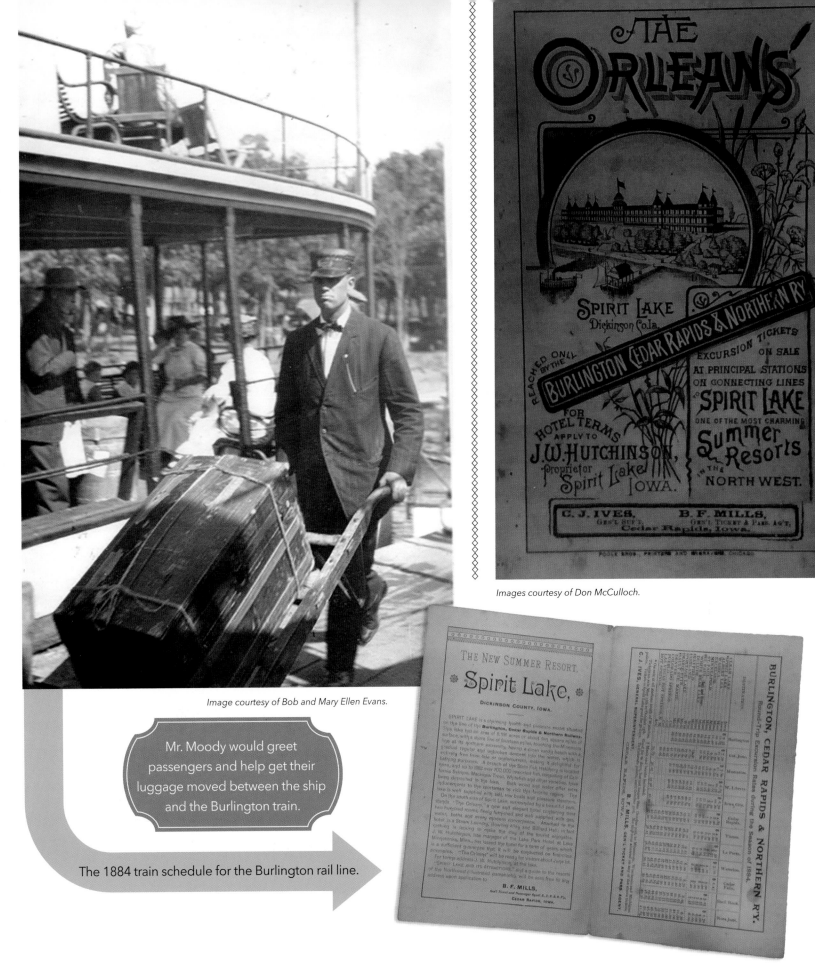

Images courtesy of Don McCulloch.

Image courtesy of Bob and Mary Ellen Evans.

Mr. Moody would greet passengers and help get their luggage moved between the ship and the Burlington train.

The 1884 train schedule for the Burlington rail line.

The Chicago, Milwaukee, St. Paul Railway traveled from Spirit Lake, Okoboji, and Arnolds Park on its way to Spencer and Des Moines.

The Spirit Lake depot, the terminus of the Milwaukee line.

Image courtesy of Iowa Great Lakes Maritime Museum.

The Okoboji depot was located just north of the Grade area.

Image courtesy of Iowa Great Lakes Maritime Museum.

The train trestle at the grade would be turned to let the steamships pass.

Image courtesy of Iowa Great Lakes Maritime Museum.

This is the railroad bridge at Okoboji. Opening for boats to pass.

The Arnold's Park depot with the Okoboji Hotel and Pavilion in the background.

Image courtesy of Iowa Great Lakes Maritime Museum.

Today part of the old Spirit Lake depot is part of the Dickinson County Museum.

Image courtesy of Dickinson County Historical Society & Museum.

Train travel ended for the Burlington line on May 27, 1950, and for the Milwaukee line on April 12, 1952.

Did you know?

The original ENTER and DO NOT ENTER signs on the Milwaukee railroad trestle were painted late one night by three teenagers in 1968. Carol Crawford, Tom M. Evans, and Cris Clarke came up with the idea. Tom worked at the Place Down Under (under the Okoboji Store), and the girls would stop and hang out. The trio had noticed that boats traveling between the lakes kept vying for the closest opening, which often created boat congestion. They decided signs were needed. Calls were made to the railroad, Highway Patrol, and Lake Patrol to inquire about the jurisdiction. All three organizations said, "We don't care if they don't care." So, late one night the friends hung upside down and painted ENTER and DO NOT ENTER on the trestle. Those signs were replaced in 2003 with professional signs provided by the Water Safety Council.

Image courtesy of Jim Hedgpeth.

STEAMERS

When the trains arrived, they needed a way to get their passengers to locations around the lakes.

In 1880 the first steam-driven ship, the *Favorite*, took passengers from Arnold's Park to Spirit Lake. The second steamboat was the *Alpha*. It sailed Big Spirit Lake and was owned by the Burlington, Cedar Rapids & Northern Rail line. With the erection of the first swing bridge in 1883, larger steamships could now traverse the lakes.

The first forms of transportation on the lakes included canoes and sailboats.

Image courtesy of Dickinson Country Historical Society & Museum.

In 1884 the *Alpha* was replaced with the first steel-hulled steamship, the *Queen*, who had only one level at that time.

Image courtesy of Iowa Great Lakes Maritime Museum.

The *Queen* sailed Spirit Lake until 1900, when she was moved over the isthmus during winter to the Okobojis. During the move, the *Queen* broke through the ice. The railroad thought she had been severely damaged and sold her to the Henderson Bros, who repaired her in 1902. They sold the *Queen* to J. R. Swearinger, who in 1908 sold her to Roy and Fred Roff. (They purchased the entire Okoboji Steam Boat Company fleet.)

Image courtesy of Dickinson County Historical Society & Museum.

Boats moored, most likely in Smith's Bay. This is where the coal dock was located. It is also a natural harbor offering protection from the winds and storms.

Image courtesy of Wilson family.

The steamships would also winter in Smith's Bay.

Image courtesy of Luckybreak/Okoboji.

On July 1, 1884, the *Ben Lennox* made its first trip from Arnold's Park to Orleans. It was owned by the Chicago, Milwaukee, St. Paul Railway. (The *Ben Lennox* was later named the *Manhattan*, then taken apart and used as a pattern by Fred Roff to build the *Okoboji*.)

Image courtesy of Luckybreak/Okoboji.

The massive passenger sailboat *Falcon* next to the steamer *Okoboji*.

Image courtesy of Iowa Great Lakes Maritime Museum.

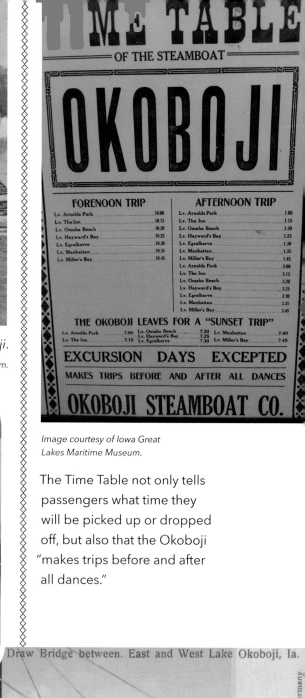

Image courtesy of Iowa Great Lakes Maritime Museum.

The Time Table not only tells passengers what time they will be picked up or dropped off, but also that the Okoboji "makes trips before and after all dances."

Passengers aboard the *Okoboji* in 1910.

Image courtesy of Iowa Great Lakes Maritime Museum.

The *Okoboji* going through the swing bridge with Arp Brothers boat works in the background. The postcard shows it was purchased by the A. O. Stevens company in Arnold's Park. This was Wesley Arnold's son-in-law and the founder of the Lakeside Department Store.

Image courtesy of Iowa Great Lakes Maritime Museum.

Draw Bridge between. East and West Lake Okoboji, Ia.

IONA

Image courtesy of the O'Farrell family.

Not all steamers were large, two-deck ships. Bert O'Farrell would take passengers aboard his steamer the *Iona*. This was a lake taxi for a family or small group.

Multiple boats vying for dock space at the Arnold's Park pier (1908).

Image courtesy of Dickinson County Historical Society & Museum.

Another view at the Arnold's Park pier.

Images courtesy of the Iowa Great Lakes Maritime Museum.

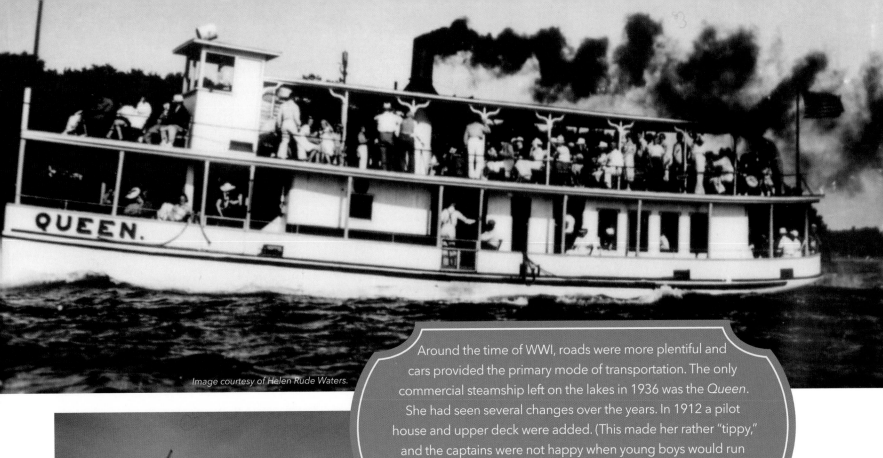

Image courtesy of Helen Rude Waters.

Around the time of WWI, roads were more plentiful and cars provided the primary mode of transportation. The only commercial steamship left on the lakes in 1936 was the *Queen*. She had seen several changes over the years. In 1912 a pilot house and upper deck were added. (This made her rather "tippy," and the captains were not happy when young boys would run from side-to-side to get her to "list".) In 1936 a new steel hull was refitted around her old one. In 1957 the *Queen* was rebuilt and converted from steam to a diesel engine.

The *Queen* sustained severe damage spring of 1971 when the ice went out.

Image courtesy of Helen Rude Waters.

The *Queen* continued to provide service until 1973, when she left the lake for Adventureland Park in Des Moines. There was a big void after she left the lake.

Image courtesy of Iowa Great Lakes Maritime Museum.

There have been other excursion boats on the lakes. In 1951 Bob Buhrow bought a boat called the *Snark*. He converted it to a paddle wheeler and renamed it the *Boji Belle*. She was taken off the lake in 1962 and used as a tourism center in Spirit Lake.

Buhrow saw the need for a larger boat, one that was more easily accessible. In May 1961 the *SS Empress* started her service. This large ship was able to handle parties with bands. She would make appointed stops at Manhattan, The New Inn, Vacation Village, and Crescent Beach. In 1983 she left the lake for Hot Springs, Arkansas.

Image courtesy of Dickinson County Historical Society & Museum.

Image courtesy of Iowa Great Lakes Maritime Museum.

Two smaller boats that provided lake tours were the *Chief* and the *Robert C.*

Image courtesy of Iowa Great Lakes Maritime Museum.

The *Robert C.*

Image courtesy of Dickinson County Historical Society & Museum and the Dickinson County News.

In the summer of 1976, a sixteenth- or seventeenth-century replica of a two-masted 53-foot brig, named the *Barracuda*, was brought to the lake by Mike Lennon. She never had her sails hoisted, but used her diesel engines for one summer, running from the Emporium. The *Barracuda* wintered in Okoboji Harbor, but was vandalized. She stayed at harbor the summer of 1977 due to mechanical problems and shallow water. In September 1977 she caught fire and was destroyed.

Image courtesy of Dickinson County Historical Society & Museum and the Dickinson County News.

After over ten years of missing the *Queen*, there was a fundraiser to build a replacement, the *Queen II*. The aluminum hull, constructed at the Palmer Johnson Shipyard of Sturgeon Bay, Wisconsin, arrived May 1986.

Image courtesy of Mary Schiltz Jensen.

The *Queen II* was christened on June 21, 1986.

Image courtesy of Iowa Great Lakes Maritime Museum.

There were two individuals that were very important to the lakes. Both were captains of a *Queen*. Roy Roff captained steamships for fifty-five years. His father, Fred Roff, helped start the Okoboji Steamboat Company in 1902. His son, Roy, began as a rope boy on the *Okoboji*. He moved to the position of captain of the *Iowa* and then of the *Queen* upon his father's retirement. Roy retired in 1962.

Captain Steve Kennedy helped lead the force to bring the *Queen II* to fruition. He was at the helm until his untimely death from cancer in February 2002. At the eulogy for Steve, close friend Ron Ames said, "It seems clear to most that the Arnolds Park Complex, including the Park, the Maritime Museum, the *Queen II*, the Green Space, the Public Beach and everything there, has become the heart and soul of the Iowa Great Lakes. I hope it is clear to all of you that Captain Steve Kennedy is the heart and soul of the Arnolds Park Complex and, what is more, I feel very certain that none of this would even exist today without him, and the Iowa Great Lakes would be drastically different. That, ladies and gentlemen, is a Legacy!"

A bright event. Before Captain Steve's passing, friends and family strung Christmas lights on the *Queen II* and took her out on a Christmas Eve cruise. The ice had not yet formed on the lake. It was a wonderful sight to see! The captain did not ride on the Christmas Eve cruise in 2001—he was too ill. He watched her with his family from his home as she stopped there for the passengers to sing carols. The lake froze over the next day.

Captain Steve Kennedy at the helm of the Queen II (circa 2000). He is fondly remembered, and his legacy to the lakes lives on in the park and museum.

Image courtesy of Iowa Great Lakes Maritime Museum.

Captain Roy Roff of the *Queen* (on the left) with Johnny Johnson and John Rude (seated), circa 1900.

Image courtesy of Helen Rude Waters.

There have been many steamships on the Iowa Great Lakes over the years. Besides those discussed here, they include the *Hiawatha, Lelia, River Queen, Iowa, Orleans, R. J. Hopkins, Chicago, Sunbeam, Des Moines, Sioux City,* and *Huntress* (renamed the *Illinois*).

Image courtesy of Iowa Great Lakes Maritime Museum.

Illinois   Okoboji   Hiawatha   Queen   Iowa   Orleans

THE OKOBOJI FLEET OF STEAMERS.

The *Queen II* is still the reigning excursion boat on West Okoboji, although boat works and a number of resorts also run excursion/bar boats.

Did you know?

There is still one steam-powered boat on Okoboji. She is called the *William Sykes* and was hand built by William Anspach. You can't help but smile when the steam whistle goes off.

Image courtesy of Okoboji Tourism and Blue Water Ventures, David Thoreson.

BOAT WORKS

If there are boats, there needs to be a place, or places, to work on them.

To truly understand the relationship between the two original boat works, a genealogy lesson is in order. Fred Roff moved to Okoboji in 1881. He was a railroad man, but started the Fred Roff Boat House on Smith's Bay. Fred had three children: Roy (who helped his father in the ship building and captained many steamships), Della (who married Charles Gipner), and Lou (she married Ed Wilson).

There are two original boat works: Okoboji Boat Works (Roff/Arp/Gipner/Okoboji Boat Works) and Mau Marine (Hendersons/Wilson Boat Works/Mau Marine). Both are located in the protected area near the grade.

Roff/Arp/Gipner/Okoboji Boat Works

Peter Arp moved to Okoboji in February 1882. He was a ships carpenter and had three sons, Arthur (A. E.), George, and Julius. George and A. E. ran the business. The boat works was started as a building and repair shop. Engines weren't using gasoline back then, so there were no gas pumps.

The big building on the current Okoboji Boat Works property on Smith's Bay was built in 1898 by the Arp brothers. Both brothers were credited with building many boats that were used on the Iowa Great Lakes. George and A. E. died in 1939, and the business was taken over by Julius Arp and neighbor B. A. O'Farrell. In 1940 it was sold to Kenneth and Charles Gipner. (They were Fred Roff's son-in-law and grandson.)

By the time Charlie Gipner took the helm of Arps Boat Works, motorboats were the rage. He renamed the business Gipner Boat Works.

Several boat owners would store their boats in a storage facility that provided them cover at Gipner's. On Saturday, July 22, 1944, a fire broke out around midnight. It was believed to be caused by an electrical short in one of the boats being stored at the boathouse. Had it not been a relatively still night, the entire beach's structures might have caught fire. There were seven boats destroyed and a couple others badly damaged.

Two neighbors, Roy Roff and Barbara Marshall, rushed into the inferno and cut loose some boats before they caught fire. Edna Mae O'Farrell and Mrs. Donald Williams went out into the water in a small rowboat using yard rakes to do their best to keep burning boats from landing near the homes and businesses. Those four were hailed as heroes. The boat storehouse was a complete loss.

In 1965 Wayne Eves, from Omaha, bought the boat works and renamed it Okoboji Boat Works. He also purchased the Central Ballroom, now known as the Central Emporium, to be used for storing boats.

In 1974 Robert (Boob) and Joani Schneider took over ownership of Okoboji Boat Works and in 1986 sold it to Jim and Diana Jensen. During their ownerships, the boat works had few changes in general operation.

In 2001 Leo (Butch) Parks purchased the business. Parks converted the old repair shop into a bar, not a use permitted by the property's special use permit. The neighbors were not happy. After a court case by the city, the bar was closed.

Image courtesy of Martha Green.

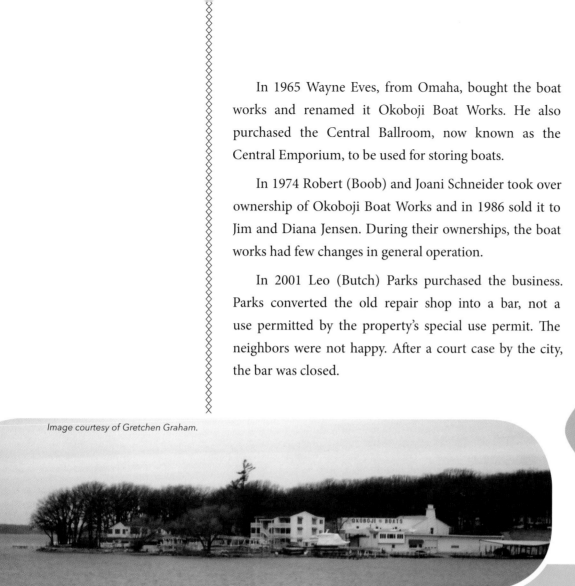

Image courtesy of Gretchen Graham.

Fred Roff started Fred Roff Boat House in 1890. He worked on boats until the gold rush lured him to Alaska in 1898. Fred rented out his shop (pictured above in 1912) to the Arp brothers, who eventually purchased it in 1914 for $2,200.

Okoboji Boat Works circa 1990s.

Okoboji Boat Works now houses a show room, gas pumps, shore shop, a swimming beach, hosts excursion boats and offers mooring for boats of all sizes.

Image courtesy of Okoboji Magazine.

Henderson/Wilson/Mau Marina

The property to the east of the grade was purchased January 14, 1895, by Henderson. He built a boat and blacksmith shop. His home was also on the property.

Image courtesy of Dickinson County Historical Society & Museum.

On February 4, 1905, the property was sold to Wilson & Sons. (W. S. Wilson had two sons, Oliver and Edward.) Wilson was very familiar with the property because in 1887 he had purchased the neighboring general store, later renamed the Okoboji Store. Oliver managed the boat works and Edward the store and boat livery.

Image courtesy of Loraine Wilson Little.

In 1920 the business owned by the Wilsons was sold to B. R. Merrill of Des Moines. There was a rapid loss of business, and Merrill sold to Art McKinney of Arnolds Park. The business went into foreclosure, and on August 14, 1926, the Wilsons regained ownership.

Ed Wilson passed the helm to his son Fred. Fred decided to remove many of the original buildings and build new structures. In 1932 he became a representative for Chris Craft boats. "This was when our business really started to flourish," Fred said.

In 1910, Oliver Wilson decided to return to farming, so Edward took over the boat business (Ed Wilson's Boat Works is pictured in 1912). The family bought additional adjoining land, including a large storage building for storing boats.

Image courtesy of Martha Green.

Smith's Bay and
the boat works
in 1942.

During WWII, the Wilson women,
Loraine Wilson and her aunt, Mrs.
Robert Osborne, took over the
operation of Wilson Boat Works as
the men were off to war.

In May 1970, Wilson sold the boat works to Harvey DeVries of Sioux City. David DeConcini, from Colorado Springs, purchased Wilson Boat Works in 1973. It was repossessed and sold to Don Schroeder. In the fall of 1983 (Charles) Helenberg Enterprises took over ownership. Between Schroeder and Helenberg, numerous improvements were made to the business, including the purchase of adjoining property. In 1988 Dick and Donna Mau purchased Wilson Boat Works and renamed it Mau Marine.

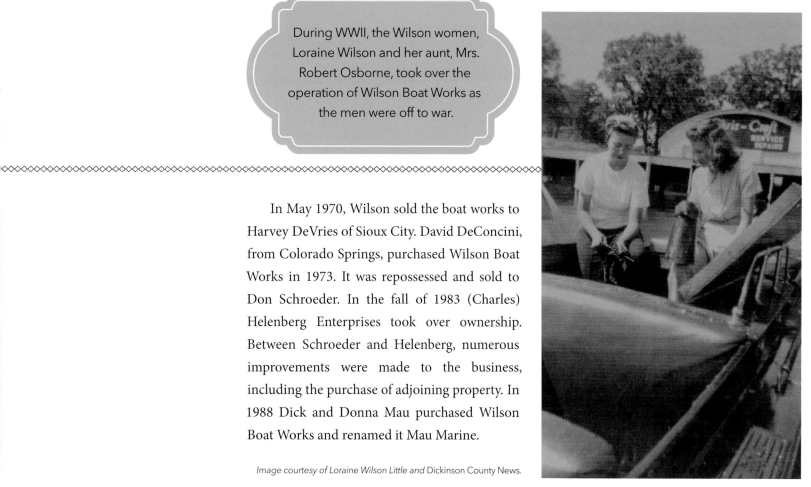

Aerial of Smith's Bay and both boat works in 2007.

Image courtesy of Brian Craig.

There are two other full-service marinas serving the lakes. Parks Marina, home of the Barefoot Bar, is located on East Okoboji. It was originally Gibson's Sporting Goods. Oak Hills Marina, on Lake Minnewashta, is the other marina.

The Mau family have updated their showrooms and added new mooring for houseboats. Their daughters, Julie and Susan, are now running the business. Doyne Wilson Hummel, Zeke Wilson's daughter, and Loraine Wilson Little, Fred Wilson's daughter, both mentioned how pleased they were that another family was passing it down within their family like theirs had done. Mau Marine is a full-service marina with sales, service, and storage of boats as well as sales of other water toys. Mooring slips and hoists are also available for lease. (2015)

Image courtesy of Mau Marine.

SAILING

The first large sailboat brought to the lake was the *Martha Washington*, owned by Crandall and Benedict, according to R.A. Smith. Many enthusiasts on Okoboji and Big Spirit were on hand for the first sailboat race, held on August 1, 1876, with six entries. B. B. Van Steenburg spearheaded the race and offered $25 in prize money. The race course was from one end of West Okoboji to the other and back again. The second race was held six weeks later, with four boats in contention. Additional boats were added to the "fleet" the summer of 1877.

Image courtesy of the Okoboji Yacht Club.

The first Okoboji Yacht Club (OYC) was formed in 1878, but didn't last long. In 1897 it was re-formed and has been located at different sites over its life.

In 1982 the OYC celebrated its fiftieth anniversary. They purchased a ten-acre tract on Miller's Bay with a 300-foot shoreline. The OYC moved in and installed their traditional Y-shaped dock. They also installed a crane to help with putting sailboats in and out. For the sailing enthusiasts, the lake often hosts multilake regattas. Today the OYC is a thriving organization for sailing and socializing.

The *Nymph* was one of the early excursion sailboats on the lake.

In 1897 the Okoboji Yacht Club re-formed. This time they had a grand building as their clubhouse. In 1892, D. C. Patterson and J. E. Baum of Omaha purchased 15.65 acres of lakeshore property. High on the bank they built a replica of the United States Treasury building as their home. (It was later considered to be haunted.) They also built a clubhouse/dining pavilion down by the water and several other small cottages for their resort community. It was the pavilion that the yacht club moved over the water. They also added to it a surrounding porch. This became THE social hub of the lake. Sailing unfortunately lost favor, and the yacht club once again disbanded. The building was torn down in the 1920s.

Image courtesy of Dickinson County Historical Society & Museum.

The 1901 OYC silver trophy.

Image courtesy of Okoboji Yacht Club.

Image courtesy of Dickinson County Historical Society & Museum.

The OYC may have disbanded, but sailing continued, and in the early 1930s the Okoboji Yacht Club was again active. At first they used Fort Dodge Point as their headquarters (which made sense, as so many members lived on Des Moines Beach or Dixon's Beach, both flanking Fort Dodge Point).

Image courtesy of Okoboji Yacht Club.

A flag would be flown on the point indicating a race. The Fort Dodge buoy would be used, as were the buoys off Gull, Manhattan, Atwell, and Pillsbury points as parts of the race course.

Image courtesy of Okoboji Yacht Club.

After the building of the Gull Point State Park Lodge in 1935, the OYC began to use that location as their headquarters. Here the boats are awaiting a race.

The next "home" of the Okoboji Yacht Club was a small building on the grounds of The New Inn, built in August 1957. This was a tiny structure, just large enough to hold the race buoys and have a classroom for their students. Races were held on Wednesday afternoons and Saturday and Sunday mornings. Classes of boats raced in the 1960s included the "C" (20-foot scow), "M20" (20-foot scow with a spinnaker or balloon sail), "M16" (16-foot scow), and the "X" (16-foot chined boat for those sailors under sixteen years of age).

Image courtesy of Okoboji Yacht Club.

The circa 1982 OYC building on Miller's Bay was torn down and a new building was built and opened in September 1997. Sailboat races now occur on Saturday and Sunday mornings. Classes of boats being raced include the "C," "MC" (16-foot with a single sail, which can be sailed by one person), "X," and "Yngling" (20-foot cross between a dinghy and keelboat, great for new sailors).

Image courtesy of Okoboji Yacht Club.

The OYC Sailing School is a wonderful way to introduce young children to the love of sailing, and you don't have to provide your own boat for the class.

Image courtesy of Okoboji Tourism and Blue Water Ventures, David Thoreson.

A picturesque weekend sailboat race on West Okoboji.

Image courtesy of Okoboji Tourism and Blue Water Ventures, David Thoreson.

BATH HOUSE

BATHING
ARNOLD PARK
IA

5

ARNOLDS PARK

Many of the first white settlers to own land in the Arnolds Park region were killed in the massacre of 1856. They included the Gardner and Luce families. The Wilsons also owned property. All this land was later purchased by the Rev. J. S. Prescott, who was a Methodist preacher. He made the first improvements in 1857–1858. Prescott's original home became a popular stopping place for campers. He sold some of this land to Wesley B. Arnold from Wisconsin in 1864.

Arnold was an astute businessman and saw great potential in the property on the shore of West Okoboji. If he saw a need, he built what was needed. In 1874 he opened his home for tenting parties.

In 1882 young Hattie Arnold, Wesley's daughter, was swinging in a hammock with Ada Lewis, the daughter of a conductor on the Milwaukee railroad. The girls were talking about how lovely and park-like the property was. They decided to call it "Arnold's Park." The name stuck, but the apostrophe was later removed.

So we now have a name for the area, with vacationers coming, new train service, but not much more. Swimming was of course popular, and bathers could rent a swimming outfit for the day. For 25 cents they would get a bucket with a swimsuit in it. They would go into the bathing house to change, put their street clothes in the bucket, and the operators would watch the belongings. (One wonders just how large these buckets/baskets must have been to hold all the clothes a fashionable woman wore at the time.)

In 1882 W. B. Arnold began the construction of the Arnold's Park Hotel. It was located to the southeast of the current amusement park.

Images courtesy of Iowa Great Lakes Maritime Museum.

In 1889, the first amusement ride was added to the Arnolds' property. This was a toboggan waterslide. Revelers would haul a toboggan to the top of a large slide—and whoosh!

Image courtesy of Iowa Great Lakes Maritime Museum.

Arnold hit it big, and in 1901 he built a pavilion for dancing (the large building behind the boat office). The pavilion could hold 1,000 chairs and had a stage as well. Arnold's Park was quite the draw. According to R. A. Smith in *The History of Dickinson County Iowa*, "Anything and everything that tends to attract and interest a promiscuous crowd is found here in abundance."

Image courtesy of the Dickinson County Historical Society & Museum.

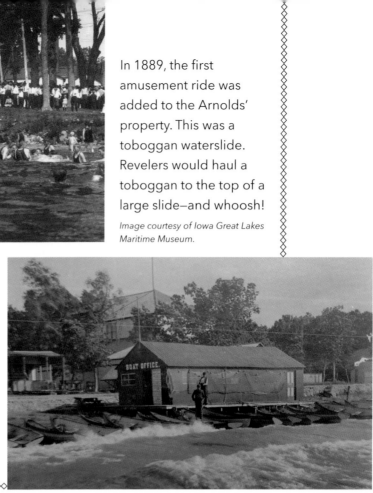

Arnold and his son-in-law A. O. Stevens developed the Lakeside Department Store. Sadly, on October 20, 1905, Wesley Arnold passed away. The property was passed on to his three daughters Hattie, Ella, and Mable.

Image courtesy of Iowa Great Lakes Maritime Museum.

History gets a bit confusing at this point about just who owned what, and when and which improvements were made to each park. For the ease of telling the story, the park will be divided into two sections. From the lake, looking at the State Pier and main road, everything on the right went to Ella Arnold Stevens and her sister Mable Arnold Bardon of Texas. Everything on the left went to Hattie Arnold Peck (later Sanford). Improvements were made on both the properties.

In 1918 the Stevens/Bardon lakeshore property was sold to C. P. Bennit. This half now was called Bennit's Amusement Park. In 1919 the Majestic Roller Rink opened at Bennit's. They also provided a shooting gallery, gypsy fortune-teller, and an airplane swing. There was also a large involvement by gypsies in the day-to-day operations of the parks far into the 1980s.

The most significant change to the site came in 1923. This was the year the second story was added to the Lakeside Department Store. This space was named the "Roof Garden" and was the second largest dance hall in the country. It hosted big names such as Tommy Dorsey, Glenn Miller, and Louis Armstrong. Often dancers were so active, the floor could be felt bouncing.

Times and music trends change, and the first rock-and-roll band played at the Roof Garden in 1955 under the ownership and management of Darlowe Oleson.

Image courtesy of Iowa Great Lakes Maritime Museum.

Entry to Stevens Beach.

View of Arnold's Park, Ia. from Lake Okoboji

Steven's Beach, Lake Okoboji, Iowa.

A good view of the Lakeside Department Store, the dance pavilion, and Stevens Beach building.

Image courtesy of Iowa Great Lakes Maritime Museum.

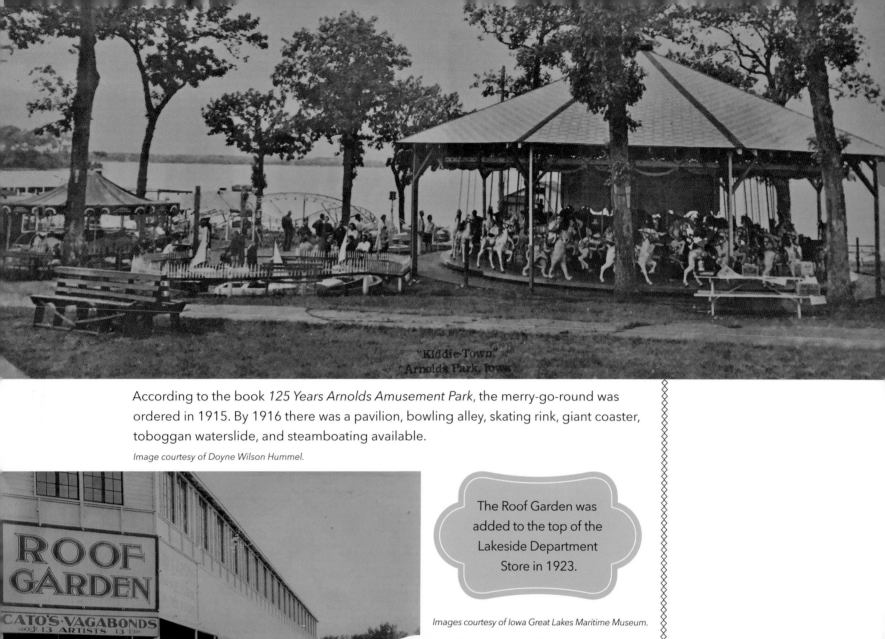

"Kiddie-Town"
Arnolds Park, Iowa

According to the book *125 Years Arnolds Amusement Park*, the merry-go-round was ordered in 1915. By 1916 there was a pavilion, bowling alley, skating rink, giant coaster, toboggan waterslide, and steamboating available.

Image courtesy of Doyne Wilson Hummel.

The Roof Garden was added to the top of the Lakeside Department Store in 1923.

Images courtesy of Iowa Great Lakes Maritime Museum.

Activity at the docks at Arnolds Park in the 1920s.

Image courtesy of Don McCulloch.

Image courtesy of Don McCulloch.

In 1927 the sea wall was built to allow lakeside automobile parking. The original pavilion was turned into the Fun House in 1929.

The Giant Dips Roller Coaster was built in 1930, later known as the Speed Hound, and finally the Legend. The Tipsy House and State Pier were also added that year.

Image courtesy of Iowa Great Lakes Maritime Museum.

View looking past the Roof Garden, 1938.

Image courtesy of Don McCulloch

Beach fun in the 1940s.

Image courtesy of Iowa Great Lakes Maritime Museum.

The Roof Garden as it looked in the 1950s, with the old pavilion, now Fun House, on the right.

Image courtesy of Iowa Great Lakes Maritime Museum.

Roller skaters at the Majestic circa 1950.

Image courtesy of Iowa Great Lakes Maritime Museum.

EMPRESS
TICKETS
HERE
fresh up
MIDWAY
BOAT RIDES
ROOT BEER

Image courtesy of O'Farrell family.

Waterfront in the 1960s.

Fun at the amusement park circa 1965.

Image courtesy of Libby Diers Anderson.

Roof Garden promotions (poster from August 1966, a pocket card from June 1968, and band posters).

Images courtesy of Tom Tourville–Midwest Publications.

HEAD EAST
In Concert
Wed. July 9th
The Roof Gardens
Arnold's Park, Okoboji Lake
Doors Open at 7 p.m.
Tickets $7.00 Advance $8.00 Day of Show
Tickets on Sale Now At: The Roof Garden, 3 Sons Milford, Ryan's Musicland, Spencer and Estherville, Lusk Music, Jackson, MN. And Musicland, Worthington, MN.

Dance to the fabulous
Flippers
Listen for them on KOMA
ROOF GARDEN
SUNDAY, SEPT. 5
Last Dance of the Season
8-12
Adm. $1.50

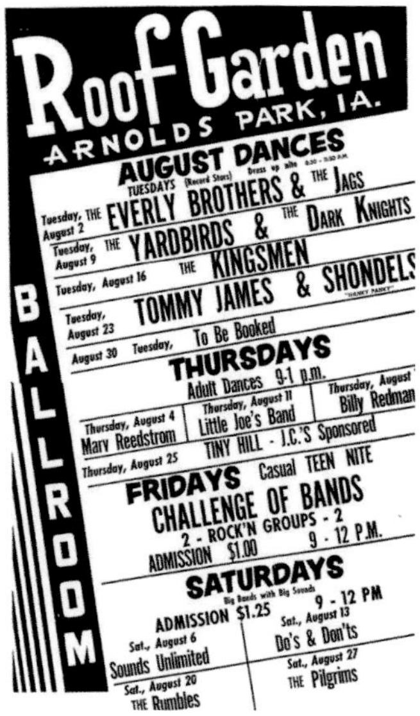
Roof Garden
ARNOLDS PARK, IA.
BALLROOM
AUGUST DANCES
TUESDAYS (Record Stars)
Tuesday, August 2 THE EVERLY BROTHERS & THE JAGS
Tuesday, August 9 THE YARDBIRDS & THE DARK KNIGHTS
Tuesday, August 16 THE KINGSMEN
Tuesday, August 23 TOMMY JAMES & SHONDELS
August 30 Tuesday, To Be Booked
THURSDAYS
Adult Dances 9-1 p.m.
Thursday, August 4 Mary Reedstrom
Thursday, August 11 Little Joe's Band
Thursday, August Billy Redman
Thursday, August 25 TINY HILL - J.C.'S Sponsored
FRIDAYS Casual TEEN NITE
CHALLENGE OF BANDS
2 - ROCK'N GROUPS - 2
ADMISSION $1.00 9 - 12 P.M.
SATURDAYS
Big Bands with Big Sounds
ADMISSION $1.25 9 - 12 PM
Sat., August 6 Sounds Unlimited
Sat., August 13 Do's & Don'ts
Sat., August 20 THE Rumbles
Sat., August 27 THE Pilgrims

Roof Garden
ARNOLDS PARK, IA.
BALLROOM
JUNE ATTRACTIONS
TUESDAYS RECORD STARS
8:30 - 11:30
JUNE 4 - FABULOUS RUMBLES - ADM. $1.75
11 - BOX TOPS - ADM. $2.00
18 - BUCKINGHAMS - ADM. $2.00
25 - SPIRIT OF ST. LOUIS - ADM. $1.75
FRIDAYS
CHALLENGE OF BANDS
2 - BANDS - 2
WINNER JUDGED BY YOUR APPLAUSE
ADM. $1.00
9 - 12 P.M.
SATURDAYS TOP TERRITORY BANDS
ADM. $1.25
9 - 12 P.M.
JUNE 1 - ROYAL EMPERORS
8 - THE NOBLEMEN
15 - THE SENDERS
22 - CHURCHKEYS
29 - ALEXANDER ROCK TIME BAND

The "roofless" Roof Garden after the tornado in June 1968.

Image courtesy of Dickinson County News.

The rebuilt Roof Garden after the tornado.

Image courtesy of Iowa Great Lakes Maritime Museum.

June 13, 1968, brought disaster to much of the south end of the lake. A strong tornado went through and took the roof off the Roof Garden. Trees were uprooted and caused damage to the Legend roller coaster and other amusements.

The community got together and on July 2, the Roof(less) Garden was reopened. According to Emil Richter, the first performance in the "Roofless Garden" was Mary Lee Rush. She performed "Angel of the Morning" from the southeast corner of the space. A wooden fence had been built about eight feet from the edge of the building. One could hear the DJ saying good-night to all the revelers until the building was repaired.

The Nutty Bar stand, a favorite still today, was added in 1949. This sweet delight consists of a block of vanilla ice cream on a stick covered in chocolate and chopped peanuts. (The stand in the park is the only place you can get an original nutty bar.)

The late 1980s were not kind to the park. The highlight was the new *Queen II*, which had her inaugural voyage on June 21, 1986. However, the park visibly had seen better times. The Majestic Roller Rink was closed in 1987, and in 1988 the park was closed for a year.

The Fun House was demolished (the rides were saved, and many are now at the Boji Bay Fun House and Pavilion), and saddest of all, the Roof Garden was downed in a controlled fire burn. The building burned down faster than anyone could have imagined! Jim Carpenter, who was with the Arnolds Park Volunteer Fire Department and worked the fire, said there were seventy volunteer firefighters from seventeen different departments. The fire was HOT! It had been scheduled for an earlier date, but had been postponed due to the wind. The firefighters reported at 8:00 a.m. and started with search and rescue training.

When it came time to light the initial fire, Jim said it only took about sixty to ninety minutes from start to finish. All there agreed that had there been a fire with dancers in the Roof Garden, many would never have made it out.

The controlled burning of the Roof Garden in 1988.

Images courtesy of Keith Kennedy.

In 1989 the park was purchased by a group of investors, and in 1991 new life came to Arnolds Park with the opening of the Maritime Museum headed by *Queen II* Captain Steve Kennedy. Chuck Long purchased the property in 1996 and added the new Century Ferris Wheel.

But 1999 was a pivotal year for the amusement park. It was sold to a developer, Don Dunham, who announced it was going to be razed for a condo/resort development. The lakes community was outraged!

The "Save the Park" fundraising campaign began. What a daunting task they had, to raise $5.5 million in a six-week time span. (This was the same amount Dunham had paid for the property; he did not make money on this deal.)

By the end of the campaign, $7.25 million had been raised, and Arnolds Amusement Park was saved! When the property was sold to Dunham, the sale did not include the rides. Chuck Long had kept them and donated them back to the revived amusement park. Still more work was needed to bring the park back to a place families wanted to (re)visit.

After many, many improvements, the park was severely in debt. A new campaign, "Sustain Our Park," was held in 2005, and the debt was retired. Since that date Pirates Cove Mini Golf was added. The Legend was renovated (now the thirteenth oldest operating wooden coaster in the world), and the Majestic Pavilion was brought back to life hosting Big Band music. Its name…the Roof Garden!

The new Okoboji Spirit Center was built to house the much enlarged Maritime Museum as well as a Welcome Center, Iowa Great Lakes Area Chamber of Commerce Chamber, and the then University of Okoboji Foundation (now Okoboji Foundation) and Okoboji Tourism offices.

Image courtesy of Explore Okoboji.

Iowa Rock 'n Roll Museum at Arnolds Park.

Image courtesy of Explore Okoboji.

The public pier now has a statue in honor of Captain Steve Kennedy. (Note the young boy with his iconic nutty bar.)

Image courtesy of Iowa Great Lakes Maritime Museum.

Aerial shot of Arnolds Park 2015. Arnolds Park, the amusement park and town, is the place to be for activities. Even today, within a two-block space, visitors find a school, a bible conference ministry, and a gentlemen's club, and everyone gets along. If you want to find most any kind of diversion, Arnolds Park is the place to go then and now.

Image courtesy of Okoboji Tourism and Blue Water Ventures, David Thoreson.

Before lovely cottages and businesses were built, visitors would stay in organized camps. This tent community was typical of the early years at Okoboji. It was located on Pillsbury Point.

Image courtesy of Iowa Great Lakes Maritime Museum.

GEMS OF THE LAKE

6

Okoboji is natural beauty, but it is also the places and people that inhabit it that make it special. Some of the places mentioned are no longer in existence. Fire has taken some, and others were just demolished. But these gems still need to be remembered.

Then there were the simple cottages. Some were owned and others rented (1966).

Image courtesy of Lesleigh Buck.

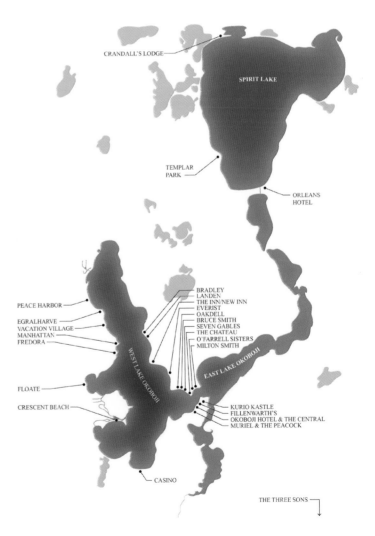

Follow along using this map that shows locations of the gems of the lake discussed in this chapter.

Image courtesy of State of Iowa GIS and Leslie Suhr

RESORTS AND HOTELS

Camping led to cabins and hotels and eventually resorts and mansions. This book is primarily about West Okoboji, but the story of the magnificent resorts and hotels starts at Big Spirit Lake.

ORLEANS HOTEL

At the end of the nineteenth century, the railroads were the driving force behind populating a location—in the days of grand hotels. The Burlington, Cedar Rapids & Northern Railway Company had just been completed to the isthmus between East Okoboji and Big Spirit Lake the summer of 1882. The railroad men were convinced Big Spirit Lake was the lake of the area with its deep, sandy beaches. What they didn't know was the water level in 1882 was the highest known at the time, and a drought was on the way.

The Burlington railroad built a magnificent structure. The original Orleans Hotel was opened to the public June 16, 1883. It was an impressive destination—324 feet by 40 feet with three stories on one end and two on the other, nine towers and a spacious dining room. The bedrooms all had a door to the hall and one to the long porches, with all the modern conveniences including baths.

The gala opening of the Burlington Railway's Hotel Orleans in 1883 was attended by many dignitaries. This was "the place" for the wealthy from New York to visit, as Prohibition had yet to impact Iowa.

Image courtesy of Don McCulloch.

This location seemed to be jinxed. The New Hotel Orleans was erected by John Burmister in 1906. The hotel was leveled by fire January 28, 1908. It was rebuilt starting in 1908 but burned on May 10, 1909, before it was finished. Orders were given to rebuild the structure with the same plans. It was opened in August 1909 (image from 1911).

Image courtesy of Luckybreak/Okoboji.

However, the lake waters receded due to drought. Then the state of Iowa passed prohibition of alcohol in 1894.

By 1898 the lakes had dropped eight feet. Steamships could no longer travel up East Okoboji and had a hard time navigating Big Spirit. On August 19 a major storm damaged the hotel. Instead of repairing it, this beautiful marvel was torn down, with its lumber and other building supplies going into homes in the area.

The last New Hotel Orleans also met with a fiery death on July 3, 1936. After that a much smaller motel was built, then later torn down. There is now a residence on the property.

CRANDALL'S LODGE

As quoted from a Burlington railroad booklet in *History of Dickinson County Iowa*, "Spirit Lake has many summer cottages along the shores with a few resorts where visitors are entertained. The most noted of these is Crandall's Lodge on the northwest shore. This famous place has been identified with Spirit Lake for more than thirty years and has sheltered many hunters and anglers who came here year after year to enjoy the superb hunting and fishing. There are none of the restraints of a fashionable summer resort at Crandall's Lodge, but visitors here come to have a good time unhampered by anything that will prevent the fullest enjoyment."

Besides the lodge there were several small cottages available. In 1901 there were accommodations for about eighty people.

The first lodging house built here was called Hunters Lodge, which was built in 1871. It was purchased by Orlando Crandall in 1879 who renamed it Crandall's Lodge. The old structure was torn down and a new one built on its site.

Image courtesy of Dickinson County Historical Society & Museum.

Crandall's Lodge, 1944.

Image courtesy of Don McCulloch.

Crandall's Lodge in its heyday.

Image courtesy of Iowa Great Lakes Maritime Museum.

Image courtesy of Mary Schiltz Jensen.

Crandall's Lodge, 1976, before it was torn down.

TEMPLAR PARK

Templar Park was a place for Sir Knights, a high degree of the Masons' organization, and also for their families. Cottages surrounded the initial complex were built in 1891.

The Knights Templar discussed the idea of purchasing a campground in 1883. In 1885, twenty-one acres were presented to the group—a gift from the people of Spirit Lake, the railroad, and others. In August 1890, the Knights Templar held a conclave in a tent near Big Spirit Lake.

The first buildings were erected in 1891. There was a devastating tornado on August 19, 1898, and they were destroyed. The rebuilt site was again devastated when fire took the structures on June 14, 1917.

As with many grand, old buildings, this complex came upon disuse. The buildings needed care, but due to their construction, the cost was exorbitant. The complex was left fairly idle, but the grounds were active with families in their own cottages.

The 1970s were not kind to Templar Park. In 1972 the facility was closed. A development company agreed to a long-term lease of the property with one major concession: all buildings must be moved or razed. A fight was on. Those who had built their own cottages worked hard to keep things alive. In 1976 a suit was filed to preserve the property by the Corporation for the Preservation of Templar Park.

At some point during this period, someone forgot to drain the water from the pipes for winter. The pipes burst and the cost for repairs was prohibitive. The main building was torn down in 1979.

In January 1987 the Department of Natural Resources announced they planned on buying much of Templar Park. The papers were signed on October 15, 1987. Cost to the DNR was $350,000. That area is now a public day park and boat access. Other properties are privately owned.

In 1919 a new apartment building was erected to withstand fire. It had 143 rooms. A new pavilion was also built (image from 1921).

Image courtesy of Iowa Great Lakes Maritime Museum.

Templar Park grounds in 1924 showing the old ponds in-filled for a golf course and parade grounds.

Image courtesy of Luckybreak/Okoboji.

Image courtesy of Iowa Great Lakes Maritime Museum.

Image courtesy of Iowa Great Lakes Maritime Museum.

In 1977 the site was put on the National Register of Historic Places.

THE INN/THE NEW INN

The location on the east side of the lake was first known as Maple Grove, then Bennett's Beach, then Dixon's Beach.

Maple Grove was owned by Dr. Isaac H. Harriott. Upon his death the family chose not to keep the property, so in 1858 it went to Daniel Bennett. Aaron Dixon was then deeded the property in 1867.

On August 16, 1882, Dixon sold it to a group of investors associated with the Burlington, Cedar Rapids & Northern Railway. At the time the railroads were instrumental in bringing vacationers to the lakes. These individuals had a scheme to profit by strategically having the railroad cover their costs. Two of the partners of the scheme, both associated with the railroad, President Mitchell and Superintendent Merrill, died about this time, and the plan was scrapped.

After a few other transactions, J. A. Beck bought half of the property on October 19, 1896. On August 14, 1897, he purchased the remaining half.

Beck started to build "The Inn" in 1896. It began with one building on the east knoll on the property with twenty-four rooms. He continued to build and ended up covering both knolls providing, per a 1901 ad, "77 well-ventilated and cozily furnished rooms, 57 have south, and lake, exposures." To the back of the newest addition was a large dining room and kitchen.

The Inn panorama from a postcard during the ownership of J. A. Beck.

Image courtesy of Iowa Great Lakes Maritime Museum.

General View at The Inn, Lake Okoboji, Ia.

Guests would arrive at the Okoboji depot, and a horse-drawn surrey would take them to The Inn.

Image courtesy of Doyne Wilson Hummel and Dickinson County News.

J. A. Beck had been coming to the lakes area to camp and loved this site called Dixon's Beach. He was an experienced hotel man from Fairfield, Iowa.

Image courtesy of Doyne Wilson Hummel and Dickinson County News.

J. A. Beck
Mr. J. A. Beck was the original builder and owner of the famous old Inn. The story goes that he promised his wife that he would build only a dozen units at first to see how it would go but ended up building the twenty four unit longtime landmark pictured on the top of page one this section.

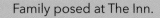

Family posed at The Inn.

Image courtesy of The New Inn.

Image courtesy of Iowa Great Lakes Maritime Museum.

e place for
g and fishing
Oscar

The Pavilion, Bazar, and The Inn with the *Queen* at the dock. Beck built the dancing pavilion in about 1900 out over the lake. The structure measured 112 by 80 feet. Above the dance floor were ten large bedrooms.

THE INN

MRS. SARAH CALLENDER
(Aunt Sarah)
Daughter Margaret Lynch

MRS. FRANK JAQUITH
(Aunt Polly)

In 1903 the Hutchins sisters, Mrs. S. T. Callendar (Aunt Sarah) and Mrs. W. Jaquith (Aunt Polly), took over the management of The Inn as their summer "vacation." This was going to be a one-year stint. In 1910 they purchased the property. In 1927 the pavilion was remodeled and enclosed.

Image courtesy of Doyne Wilson Hummel and Dickinson County News.

The "Spoon Holder," a place where adults could be childlike, at The Inn, with the pavilion in the background.

Image courtesy of Iowa Great Lakes Maritime Museum.

The Inn mid-1900s.

Image courtesy of The New Inn.

The Beach Club at The Inn.

Image courtesy of The New Inn.

Owner Sanford announced The Inn would not be opened for the 1954 season. The Inn was razed and The New Inn arose on the site. The New Inn was a series of one-story units for rent along the lakeshore. Up the hill from these lakeshore units was a main building containing dining facilities and the main office. An outside pool was also included in the plans. Over the years many improvements were added to the extensive site. An indoor pool building, par 3 golf course, conference facilities, gift shop, and many support buildings have been built. One of the favorite groups the locals loved to have visit were regional cheerleader camp groups. It was fun to walk by and see all the kids practicing on the golf course and how they had decorated their windows and doors.

The State Conservation Commission ordered the pavilion at The Inn removed in 1936, as they did not want structures over the water. Like other establishments, this one also had fire problems. On September 26, 1934, a fire had broken out in a room above the kitchen. The fire leveled the dining room of the old hotel. The Inn garage was turned into a tearoom, and life went on.

On October 5, 1944, the Hutchins sisters signed papers to sell The Inn to A. R. Johnson of Sioux Falls. This sale did not include the Inn Cottage, where the sisters resided. Later that day, Jaquith awoke from a nap to find her curtains on fire. By the time the fire departments arrived, the building was a total loss.

A. R. Johnson took possession of The Inn in May 1945. Johnson ran The Inn until it was sold to Art Sanford of Sioux City in the spring of 1954. Sanford tore down the old structures and built The New Inn on the site.

In 1999 David Slattery from Omaha purchased The New Inn. He worked to update the property. In 2011 the property was transferred to a new owner, and on December 27, 2013, it became the property of Central Bank and is being managed by the DePalma Hotels & Resorts.

This summer of 2016 marks the sixtieth straight year Marilyn Maye will be performing. She is a wonderful classic singer and Inn icon.

Image courtesy of Fred Cerwick.

"Traditions begin where memories are made." The New Inn (in 2015) has so very many traditions and memories!

VACATION VILLAGE/VILLAGE WEST

Vacation Village was the dream child of Hobart Ross.

The Ross family had roots in Okoboji. They had previously purchased the grand old Manhattan Hotel and totally reworked that property. In 1948 Hobart Ross purchased 68 acres of farmland on the west shore to create the perfect family resort. Twenty acres were used for their plan. Hobart and his sons, Robert (Bob) and Keith, built the resort, including a cottage for Hobart's parents. The property became the permanent residences for the men and their families.

When Vacation Village opened in 1949 there were ninety-one units. These consisted of one-, two-, and four-bedroom cabins.

Image courtesy of Dickinson County Historical Society & Museum.

Aerial photograph of Vacation Village, circa 1960.

Image courtesy of the Ross family.

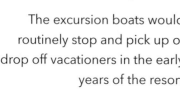

The excursion boats would routinely stop and pick up or drop off vacationers in the early years of the resort.

Image courtesy of the Ross family.

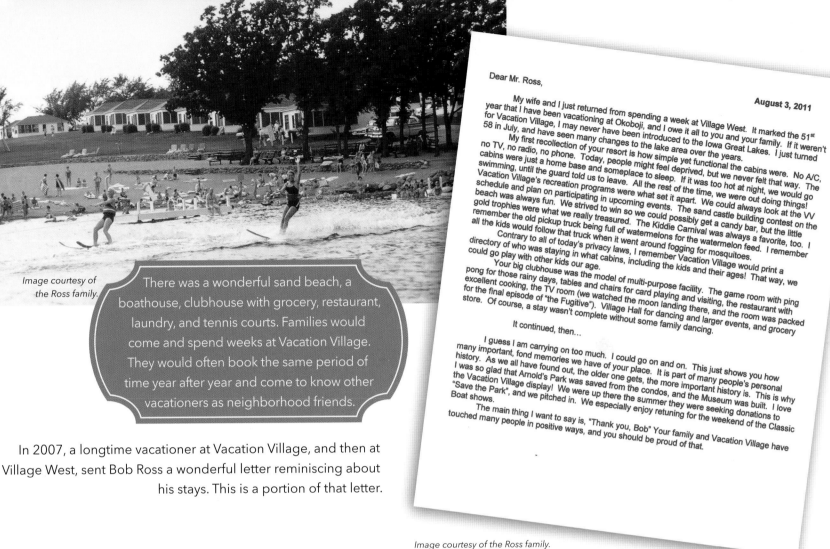

Image courtesy of the Ross family.

There was a wonderful sand beach, a boathouse, clubhouse with grocery, restaurant, laundry, and tennis courts. Families would come and spend weeks at Vacation Village. They would often book the same period of time year after year and come to know other vacationers as neighborhood friends.

In 2007, a longtime vacationer at Vacation Village, and then at Village West, sent Bob Ross a wonderful letter reminiscing about his stays. This is a portion of that letter.

August 3, 2011

Dear Mr. Ross,

My wife and I just returned from spending a week at Village West. It marked the 51st year that I have been vacationing at Okoboji, and I owe it all to you and your family. If it weren't for Vacation Village, I may never have been introduced to the Iowa Great Lakes. I just turned 58 in July, and have seen many changes to the lake area over the years.

My first recollection of your resort is how simple yet functional the cabins were. No A/C, no TV, no radio, no phone. Today, people might feel deprived, but we never felt that way. The cabins were just a home base and someplace to sleep. If it was too hot at night, we would go swimming, until the guard told us to leave. All the rest of the time, we were out doing things! Vacation Village's recreation programs were what set it apart. We could always look at the VV schedule and plan on participating in upcoming events. The sand castle building contest on the beach was always fun. We strived to win so we could possibly get a candy bar, but the little gold trophies were what we really treasured. The Kiddie Carnival was always a favorite, too. I remember the old pickup truck being full of watermelons for the watermelon feed. I remember all the kids would follow that truck when it went around fogging for mosquitoes.

Contrary to all of today's privacy laws, I remember Vacation Village would print a directory of who was staying in what cabins, including the kids and their ages! That way, we could go play with other kids our age.

Your big clubhouse was the model of multi-purpose facility. The game room with ping pong for those rainy days, tables and chairs for card playing and visiting, the restaurant with excellent cooking, the TV room (we watched the moon landing there, and the room was packed for the final episode of "the Fugitive"). Village Hall for dancing and larger events, and grocery store. Of course, a stay wasn't complete without some family dancing.

It continued, then...

I guess I am carrying on too much. I could go on and on. This just shows you how many important, fond memories we have of your place. It is part of many people's personal history. As we all have found out, the older one gets, the more important history is. This is why I was so glad that Arnold's Park was saved from the condos, and the Museum was built. I love the Vacation Village display! We were up there the summer they were seeking donations to "Save the Park", and we pitched in. We especially enjoy retuning for the weekend of the Classic Boat shows.

The main thing I want to say is, "Thank you, Bob." Your family and Vacation Village have touched many people in positive ways, and you should be proud of that.

Image courtesy of the Ross family.

Bob Ross, Hobart's son, told the *Spirit Lake Beacon* newspaper on June 29, 1978, "Anything they ask for we try to provide—except TV, phones, air conditioning, or carpet."

In 1984 Vacation Village was sold to CHW, Inc. The property was then sold to Long Lines Ltd. in 1985. Vacation Village was extensively remodeled and renamed Village West. In 1989 the Sunrise Cove program, which converted some of the units to timeshare weeks to be sold to vacationers, was started.

The property changed hands to a large corporation in 1995 and was immediately placed for sale. In 1998 Mike Hoeppner (the H in CHW from the 1984 ownership, and owner of Executive Land Investments Co. in Okoboji) was asked if he would be interested. Hoeppner formed Iowa Resort Holdings LLC, and purchased the resort and farm on August 2, 2000.

Areas of the resort were closed after Labor Day 2000, and extensive renovations, coupled with new construction, were started. By the spring of 2001 renovations were completed, and the resort reopened. Village West now had an additional fifty hotel rooms, meeting rooms, and a variety of two-, three-, and four-bedroom timeshare units added. Additional units have been added since 2001 with room to expand. Iowa Resort Holdings LLC owns over 100 acres where the resort currently is located. During the season, the resort sleeps around 1,500 people per night.

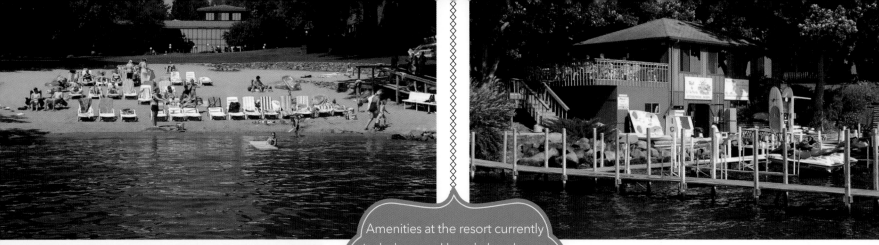

Amenities at the resort currently include a sand beach, boathouse, fuel for boats, rentals, convention facility, dining, in-house movie theater, three swimming pools, game room, and gift shop.

Images courtesy of Mike Hoeppner.

Village West is the largest resort on West Lake Okoboji. Owner Mike Hoeppner said his friends, Bob and Keith Ross, started a wonderful family resort, and it is his intent to carry on that tradition into the future.

Image courtesy of Mike Hoeppner.

MANHATTAN BEACH

Manhattan Beach was the place for the wealthy vacationers, but it was difficult to get to.

Original owner, D. B. Lyons, also purchased the *Ben Lennox* steamship and renamed it *Manhattan*. This ship would shuttle guests to and from the Arnold's Park depot in the late 1890s. The ship was old, however, and had to be removed from service in 1898. Sadly, the large dance pavilion also had to be removed due to foundation problems caused by winter's ice.

Part of the overall plan included the creation of several cottages and lots. Sadly, that venture did not work out. Guests went elsewhere and the lots didn't sell. The property went into receivership. For a while the property was revived, but once again failed.

Past owners, the Ross family, and current owner, Chuck Long, provided much of the information about Manhattan Beach.

Carl Ross, grandson of Hobart Ross (developer of Vacation Village), said, "Grampa bought it in 1933 during the Great Depression when it was in bankruptcy. He and his little family were staying at the old hotel, and a fellow asked him what he thought the place would be worth. Grampa said around $18,000, and the fellow asked if he would make that a formal offer. Grampa did and the fellow, who was the receiver, sent papers and the deal was done."

Grampa Ross hired men from the area who were out of work. All the lumber and nails were saved from the demolition. It then took six months to build the twenty-five cottages with lumber, windows, and furnishings from the old hotel. Manhattan Beach Resort was born in 1934.

The Manhattan Beach colony grew to about forty cottages. The property also had a wonderful playground, picnic grounds, and a clubhouse—and, of course, that magnificent sandy beach!

In 1893 D. B. Lyons from Des Moines purchased the land and its sandy point. He initially built a bathhouse with specially marked towels for rent. The sandy beach was privately owned and users having these towels assured that the proper fee had been paid. This photograph shows the original bathhouse in about 1900.

Image courtesy of Dickinson County Historical Society & Museum.

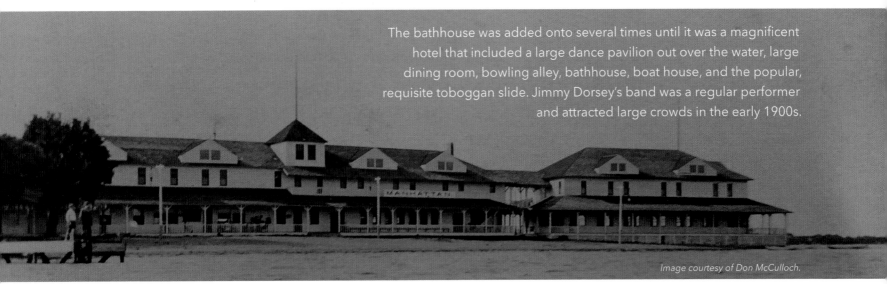

The bathhouse was added onto several times until it was a magnificent hotel that included a large dance pavilion out over the water, large dining room, bowling alley, bathhouse, boat house, and the popular, requisite toboggan slide. Jimmy Dorsey's band was a regular performer and attracted large crowds in the early 1900s.

Image courtesy of Don McCulloch.

MANHATTAN BEACH COTTAGES
W. LAKE OKOBOJI   6607

"We purchased the resort in late 1983 from Dick and Linda Fedora who were living on the property and managing the operations," said current owner Chuck Long. Originally, the future plan was to tear down all of the buildings and offer waterfront house lots for sale. Since the resort had booked reservations for the next summer, it was decided to operate it "as is" until the following fall when the resort closed for the winter and destruction could commence.

"By the time fall rolled around, the house lot plan was tossed because we became acquainted with the great group of guests that had vacationed at the resort for many years," Long said. The decision was made to bring the resort up to modern vacationer expectations, continue the family cabins, and extensively remodel the beach hotel that had been erected in the 1950s.

One of the most important parameters was not to harm any of the beautiful red oak trees that were scattered about the property by protecting them from damage. Old mattresses were strapped about the base of each oak. Excavations for installation of new utilities also avoided tree roots.

Since the 1980s, the resort continues to upgrade facilities to vacationer expectations. Although the original operations leased units by day, week, or month, the resort recently changed to full-year leasing only. This brought stability to the resort because there is very little guest turnover each year.

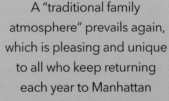

A "traditional family atmosphere" prevails again, which is pleasing and unique to all who keep returning each year to Manhattan Beach Resort.

CRESCENT BEACH

Crescent Beach was a development by J. A. Beck and H. E. Mills to help promote Lakewood Park. They had purchased 1,000 acres of land in 1911 between Emerson and Miller's Bays for a project they called Lakewood Park. The park was to be a new American Venice with canals linking the two bays. This project never was terribly successful.

Beck sold Crescent Beach to W. A. White from Spencer, Iowa, in 1916. The building was rented for a while and then remodeled. Nine two-room cottages were added around the site for families to rent. The large twelve-room "Grandview Cottage" was also added.

After White's death, his wife ran the resort for a short time. During WWII, operations were suspended. Crescent Beach was sold in 1945 to Mr. and Mrs. Carroll A. Lane, who renamed it Crescent Beach Lodge. They made many improvements over the next twenty years. The property now boasted forty-nine units, a convention center, and a new dining room.

The next owners were Bill and Laurie Shafer, who purchased the property in 1975. (Rikki Norton, current manager, who started working at Crescent under the Shafers, provided the rest of the story.) The Shafers ran the resort for about thirty years. It was a great family place, and toward the end of their ownership, they added a wonderful restaurant that is remembered for their Sunday brunches. (Even though it has been closed for years!)

In about 2006, the Shafers sold Crescent Beach to Greg Deman from Sioux City. He had planned to turn the property into timeshares, but the Town of Wahpeton would not permit this. Instead, he broke the property up, and in about 2008 sold it in three parcels.

The Nortons, from the Ames area, purchased the "Flying Cloud" four-plex condo and the "Little Sioux" cottage. The "Thunderbird Lodge," which had been closed at the time, was sold to a group of investors, Kneip, LLC. They later purchased the two other parcels from the Nortons. The restaurant was sold and became a private home.

In order to entice people to Lakewood Park, J. A. Beck's new development, he built a hunting lodge in 1914 and named it the Crescent Beach Hotel.

Image courtesy of Iowa Great Lakes Maritime Museum.

Images courtesy of Crescent Beach Lodge.

The current owners of Crescent Beach Lodge provide a family atmosphere with lakeside units and tons of amenities: playground, mini golf, Kids Kamp, sandy beach, paddle boats, great fishing, and various water sport items for rent. Crescent Beach now has twenty-seven units that can sleep from four to fourteen.

FILLENWARTH BEACH RESORT

Arthur T. Fillenwarth and his wife, Sadie, purchased land in Arnolds Park in 1918. He built a simple cottage for his family, with no windows, but awnings and screens. They named it "Old Faithful." One day a man asked to rent it, so A.T. moved his family back to their home in nearby Sanborn, Iowa, for the week. After receiving more rental offers, A.T. built more cottages for rent. (This way his family could stay at the lake.)

A.T. and Sadie had three children, but only Ken survived childhood. Ken Fillenwarth was brought up working at the "Beach Cottages" during the summer months. He would take guests out in his outboard motor rowboat and later taught water skiing. With interruptions from college years due to service in WWII, Ken completed law school, following in his father's footsteps. There he met his wife, Ruth, also an attorney. They practiced law in Estherville, Iowa, but continued to help with the resort during the summer. Ken and Ruth had two daughters, Lynn and Julie, who were also raised working at the resort during the summer months.

The first new bit of construction began in 1964, which was the Fillenwarth Beach office. Sadie died that December and never saw it completed in the spring of 1966.

Devastation hit the resort June 13, 1968. Fillenwarth Beach was destroyed by a tornado. It took out all seven upper cottages, but the lake bank units, office, and "Old Faithful" were left standing. In the fall of 1968, construction began on the large chateau building.

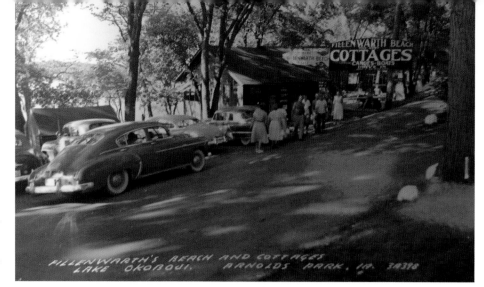

A.T. Fillenwarth first built seven cottages, then an additional twelve on the lake bank below the others. By 1930 he had thirty-six cottages.

Image courtesy of Don McCulloch.

The 1970s saw major changes to Fillenwarth's resort, business-wise and personally. Sadly, A.T. passed away in December 1971. The addition of Fillenwarth South Beach occurred in 1974, and in 1978 the old Gateswood Resort was added as The Cottage Colony. The original "Old Faithful" was given a new lease on life as an indoor pool.

Ken continued to operate the resort with assistance from Julie, while Lynn and her husband, Rich, practiced law with Ruth in Estherville, Iowa. Ruth died in 2006, and Ken in 2014. Julie now manages the property with assistance from Lynn and talented resort associates. They plan to continue the Fillenwarth operation for many years to come.

Image courtesy of Fillenwarth Beach Resort.

Fillenwarth Beach offers many options for lodging and entertainment. Watching their big sailboat taking visitors on a cruise is a joy to see. There are also water skiing lessons available, as well as sunset cruises on the *Sun Runner*.

Image courtesy of Fillenwarth Beach Resort.

> Over the years additional cottages have been added to the Fillenwarth holdings. You can always tell if it is a Fillenwarth property by the redwood siding, and especially by the strong orange trim.

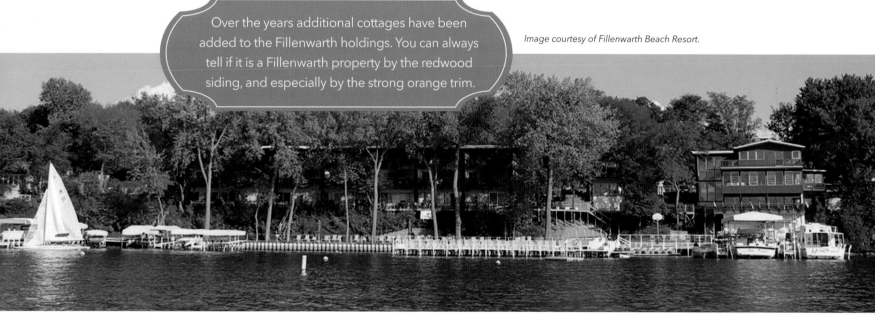

BUSINESSES

Restaurants were not going to be included in the book as they change too often. However, O'Farrell is such a landmark name, it demands attention.

O'FARRELL SISTERS RESTAURANT

Charlie Gipner built a structure directly across from the Okoboji Store to house his fishing interests. Newt Carson owned the building. The first restaurant on the upper level was called Carl's Place. It was run by Ike Kissinger.

Edna Mae and Arlene O'Farrell used to work there. When Ike decided to run for sheriff, the O'Farrells took over the restaurant, around 1947. Arlene married in 1955 and moved away. Edna Mae and sister Ferne continued to run the restaurant. In 1958 Newt decided to up the rent. It was more than the girls were willing to pay, so their father, Bert O'Farrell, built them a restaurant in the family garden plot behind their home on Smith's Bay.

O'Farrell Sisters Restaurant was known for their pancakes, fried chicken, and fish, and especially for their pies. Ferne died in 1974 and Edna Mae in 1978. The restaurant was sold to nieces Joyce Gapinski, Jo Ann Anderson, Charlotte Sarvie, and Cheri Petersen. After Jo Ann and Cheri's deaths, the remaining two decided to sell in 2003.

Butch Parks purchased the property. Customers missed having an O'Farrell at the helm, so Butch enticed Sharon Anderson London back to help make those wonderful pies.

Opening day of O'Farrell Sisters, spring 1959, (left to right) Edna Mae O'Farrell, nieces Sharon and Linda Anderson, and school friend Marvelyn Sander.

The famous O'Farrell pie recipe!

Images courtesy of O'Farrell family.

The new restaurant was built behind the O'Farrell house in their garden. The building went from lot line to lot line (which is why there is little to no parking there).

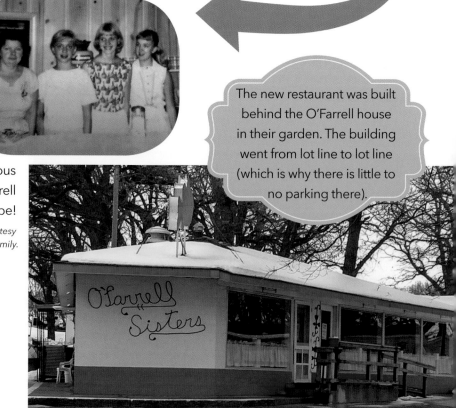

Image courtesy of Cristy Clarke Hedgpeth.

KURIO KASTLE

No one can help but do a double-take at this quirky building on Highway 71 in Arnolds Park. It was built by Harry Tennant and opened to the public in 1932 where the most amazing collection of animals, birds, fish, and reptiles was displayed.

Kurio Kastle circa 1932.

Image courtesy of Luckybreak/Okoboji.

The building now houses Jensen Real Estate.

Image courtesy of Jensen Real Estate.

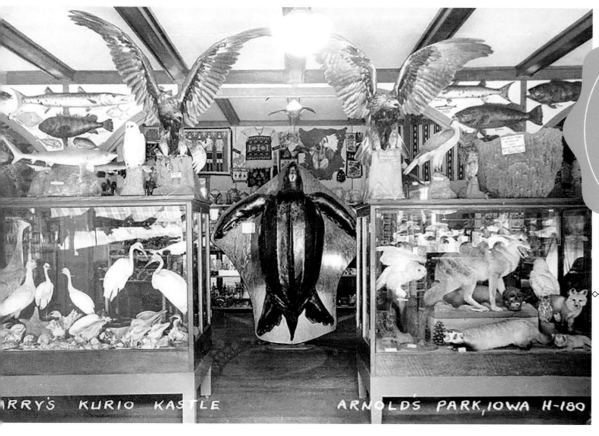

Tennant's hobby was taxidermy. When the business closed, the collection was taken by Dickinson County Conservation. Some items are viewable at the Maritime Museum in their General Store replication.

Image courtesy of Luckybreak/Okoboji.

OKOBOJI HOTEL AND THE CENTRAL EMPORIUM

Few structures, if any, have had such a varied life at Okoboji than the Emporium. But first, some history, which starts with the Okoboji Hotel.

In 1901, the Okoboji Hotel was built by the Milwaukee Railway. It was located just to the south of the Chicago, Milwaukee & St. Paul's depot. Directly behind the hotel (lakeside) was the pavilion. The Walker family of Charles City built the neighboring pavilion to serve as the hotel's dining facility on its lower level and ballroom above.

Image courtesy of Iowa Great Lakes Maritime Museum.

In 1910 Mr. Becker, from Calmer, Iowa, bought the Okoboji Hotel and Pavilion. In 1911, on August 5, the Okoboji Hotel burned to the ground. The pavilion in the background was saved due to the space between the buildings. The fire was said to have started in the basement. A bucket brigade, consisting of literally thousands of people, miraculously saved the nearby pavilion as well as the new depot.

Image courtesy of Luckybreak/Okoboji.

The Central Ballroom interior photographs.

Images courtesy of Iowa Great Lakes Maritime Museum.

Street view of the Central Pavilion after the 1911 fire.

Image courtesy of Don McCulloch

At first Becker planned on rebuilding the hotel. Instead, he added an ice cream parlor in front of the pavilion where the hotel used to be.

Image courtesy of Luckybreak/Okoboji.

Image courtesy of Iowa Great Lakes Maritime Museum.

The parlor was removed and the pavilion was renamed the Central Ballroom Nite Club. In 1926 a new brick façade was built (image circa 1927).

The Central was an amazing place in the 1920s. Howard C. Turnley operated the business. (Muriel Turnley's husband.) Musicians included Count Basie, Louie Armstrong, Glenn Miller and others. (Oh to have been there with those Big Bands!)

Courtesy pass from the Central.
Image courtesy of Rob Eves.

COURTESY PASS
Not good for Name Bands or Saturday nights
Central Ballroom
ARNOLDS PARK, IOWA
This Ticket and 50c Admits One Person
Authorized by

The Central in 1938.
Image courtesy of Don McCulloch.

GOOD NEWS! A NEW POLICY
At the Coolest Spot on the Lake!
DANCING EVERY NIGHT
CENTRAL BALLROOM
ON BEAUTIFUL LAKE OKOBOJI
Arnold's Park, Ia.
OPENS THU. JULY 21
LEXY GOLDEN and his ORCHESTRA
DANCING ALL EVENING
GENTLEMEN 40c - 10c   LADIES 10c
GEN. ADM.
DIRECT FROM THE FAMOUS CHICAGO YACHT CLUB

Dance poster from the Central Ballroom.
Image courtesy of Fred Cerwick.

The Big Band dance craze was not popular by the 1960s. In 1964 the space was rented and opened as the Golden Gaslight Theatre.
Image courtesy of Central Emporiums.

In the late 1960s, the building stood empty. Becker's family was not interested in taking over the building. In 1967 Wayne Eves, owner of Okoboji Boat Works, purchased the building to use for boat storage—an idea that didn't efficiently work. There was one large garage door, on one level only, to get boats in and out. The building had lots of columns and was built to hold people, not the weight of boats.

Eves's son, Robert, had other plans for the structure. He had spent time in San Francisco and saw what they were doing with old buildings. Ghirardelli Square and the San Francisco Cannery buildings were all the rage as new retail and dining spaces. In 1970, twenty-one-year-old Rob bought the building from his father.

So what does any intelligent young man do who now owns a massive building that needs "tender loving care"? Call his friends in to help! The bones were great, but a lot of work was needed to create the halls, shops, etc. Rob offered his college friends $1.50 an hour plus beer (IF they were twenty-one and after 4:00 p.m.) to work on the remodel. They learned how to put up stud walls, drywall, and even basic wiring. (Professionals were hired to do some of the work.) It was done with class!

Rob Eves and his pals even made the letters naming the building the "Central Emporium" (about 1971).

Image courtesy of Rob Eves.

The first year only the main level was open. Diver's Den was the first retail space on the left when entering. It was Rob's own business, relocated. Others spaces included the Outrigger restaurant (lakeside), a nautical-themed gift shop, a health food store, the candy store, and others.

Images courtesy of Rob Eves.

At the beginning there were some days the foot traffic was so slow Frisbees would be thrown in the hallway. That was only the first year. In 1972 the lower level was added and then the Bavarian Gardens bar at the very lower level, lakeside, in 1973. (The Bavarian Gardens had a waterfall with a stream and a small bridge in it. The columns had rosemaling on them in keeping with the Bavarian theme.) But now Rob was missing California.

Image courtesy of Rob Eves.

In the spring of 1975, Walter Boyle of Sioux City purchased the building. (Painting of the Emporium in 1975 by Pavonne Gipner.)
Image courtesy of Rob Eves.

In the late 1990s Dick Brown purchased the Central Emporium. He had previously rented the lower level and ran the Bavarian Gardens restaurant and bar. In 2003 Dick decided to expand the Bavarian Gardens and discovered the foundation of the structure was so bad, the building would collapse into the lake within ten years. Brown totally reinforced the building with steel columns and expanded the Gardens.

Lakeside view of the Central Emporium. One year it snowed right after Winter Games, and management was unable to gather up trash on the ice. When the ice went out, they hired divers to clean up the mess outside of the building in the lake. Now they annually send down divers to gather up discarded cans, bottles, and other items.
Image courtesy of Central Emporium.

In 2006 the "Old Girl" was sold to a private investment company. Their love of the building is strong! She is getting a new roof, and they would love to bring her looks back to the old brick façade with windows. The future looks bright for the Central Emporium.
Image courtesy of Okoboji Tourism and Blue Water Ventures, David Thoreson.

THE THREE SONS

The Three Sons, a clothing store in downtown Milford (just south of the lake), was a test market for Levi. One could always get the newest jeans there before others. If you were shopping in winter, you had to wear a coat because the only heaters were in the back room (fitting rooms) and the front room. (It has been expanded and updated since those days.)

What makes this a "gem" is that the "University of Okoboji," home of the Phantoms, was dreamed up. The Iowa Great Lakes is their campus, and "fun in life is your degree." Have you ever noticed their motto? "In God We Trust…Everyone Else Cash." They didn't accept credit cards in the store for years! Owner Emil Richter mentioned, "If the Cubs could put lights on Wrigley Field, then we could take credit cards." So they did.

This business and family have brought much to the lakes. In 1972 or '73, they placed trash cans all around the area with "Keep Our Campus Clean" stickers on the sides. In 1976 they held their first true fundraiser, and with those monies, the lakes got its first emergency extrication unit, or jaws of life. It was the second such device in the state of Iowa. The Three Sons now hosts numerous activities throughout the year. GO U of O!

Emil (left) and Herman Richter, brothers and founders of The Three Sons.

Image courtesy of Okoboji Tourism and Blue Water Ventures, David Thoreson.

The University of Okoboji actually is The Three Sons—or part of it. The Richter family boys started the business decades ago in a ramshackle building in downtown Milford. They sold various items and then hit on apparel.

Image courtesy of The Three Sons.

HOMES

Lakefront property has generally has been a good investment. In 1920 a lakefront foot cost about $100. Add a small cottage, and the total price was about $6,000. The Depression hit hard, and vacationers could get a 25-foot off-the-water lot at Triboji for $94. Between the Depression and WWII, there wasn't much selling. However, by 1960 a 50-foot lot cost between $175 to $200 per lakefront foot.

By 1980 the cost per lakefront foot reached $2,000. When the small cottages at Crescent Beach Resort were torn down, the asking price was $3,000 per foot, and they sold like hotcakes! By the early 2000s the cost was approaching $9,000, and by 2006 it was up to $12,000 per lakeside foot.

The Great Recession hit and only four houses sold. Then, in 2012 homes were selling again. During 2015 the cost per frontage foot averaged about $13,500 with the high-end lots going for almost $20,000 per foot, and the average lake cabin on a 50-foot lot costs about one million dollars.

Ever taken a leisurely evening cruise around the lake on a warm summer evening and wondered about the history of some of the cottages, cabins, and mansions? (See the map at the beginning of this chapter for locations discussed next.) These are, or were, the homes and sites that you might point to and say, "Tell me about that one."

MILTON J. SMITH HOME

Milton J. Smith arrived at the lakes in spring of 1858. Because of his military service, he was able to obtain a Military Land Warrant. That warrant was for 138.6 acres that contained all the land between West and East Okoboji, from the grade to the north where the airport road now is. Milton and his wife, Nettie, built their home on the hill overlooking Smith's Bay where the current Smith's RV business is located.

Allen Smith, great grandson of Milton, wrote "Grandma Beth said that it was operated as a boarding house for a number of years, and that governors of Iowa stayed there on their excursions to the Iowa Great Lakes. Also, my uncle Byron told me a story that was passed down to him about Cole Younger staying there overnight on his way to the Northfield Raid in 1876. At least the description: fancy horse, fancy dresser, seemed to match."

Milton J. Smith arrived shortly after his brother came to the lake as part of the contingency burying the dead from the 1856 massacre.

Image courtesy of Craig Smith.

Milton's son, Roy, took over the house at Milton's death. After Roy's death, his wife moved out and the house was left vacant. Sadly, the roof began to deteriorate, leading to other structural failures. The house had to be taken down in 1972.

Image courtesy of Bruce and Vicky Smith.

Milton built his home on the hill overlooking Smith's Bay. The home was built in 1873. (The portion on the left of the home was added when the railroad came to town.) It is this home you often see when looking at beautiful old historic lake home photographs.

THE CHATEAU

Everyone notices this property on Given's Point. It is the really colorful cottage.

Judge Given from Des Moines was the first owner when lots were sold by Milton Smith. The core of this cottage contains the first two rooms built on the shore of West Okoboji. Given had a large family. He put his sons to work. The boys first built one room, which was the kitchen. Judge Given then had his sons build a room above. The stairs were not professionally built, but are still standing strong.

The Chateau after its restoration by the Sloma family.

Image courtesy of Cristy Clarke Hedgpeth.

This is not considered to be the first "cottage" as it was more like a shack. The Givens sold it to the McHenry family of Denison in 1894.

During some of the cottage's life, Neta Seemann Redick ran a restaurant and inn on the property. This was not a lawful use, and she would frequently tell hopeful diners who would walk in off the street that she was "hosting a dinner party." Neta also had her "guests" take a stroll down the beach if she heard the police were on their way to pay her a visit.

The Chateau, named by Neta at the time she inherited it, was passed down through the family (McHenry/Seemann/Dunn/Seemann/Redick), was sold to Joseph Floyd in 1978, then to David Foxhoven in 1992. In 2000 the Sloma family bought The Chateau and did an amazing job restoring it. Neta loved color, and the Slomas brought them back with loving care. In 2013 the property was sold to Leo (Butch) Parks.

SEVEN GABLES

The first real cottage built on the shores of West Okoboji was built by George Dimmitt from Des Moines, in the 1880s. The cottage was sold to James Reaney in 1919 and twenty years later to Nelle Campbell from Oklahoma City. (The Campbells had been up visiting friends and stopped by, offered Reaney some money, and the deal was struck. The rest of the Reaney family was furious when they heard they no longer owned the cottage!)

Nelle summered there until her death in 1973. The cottage was passed on to her secretary who sold it to the Wards from Des Moines in 1975. Unfortunately it was torn down in 1998 so a year-round home could be built. The property now belongs to Dave and Jane Christ from Spencer.

Seven Gables was a true cottage. The foundation was on tree stumps, and its heating was the fireplace.

Image courtesy of Shirley Jongeward Skewis.

SMITH HOME

"The home with the stone dogs" was built by J. Q. Adams and his wife, Fannie, in 1917. The home was sturdily built, as their previous lake home had burned in 1915. (The large mansion in Spencer was also built by Adams and designed by the same architect.) In 1926 the Adamses sold the home to Nettie Wilson.

It was during the Wilsons' ownership that the concrete dog sculptures were added. The family purchased the statuary on a vacation in New Orleans, sometime around 1930. The dogs "guarded" that entry, which included a large circular drive prior to the neighboring lot being sold and built upon. In 1940, T. L. Burnight traded his smaller cottage a few doors away, plus a quarter acre of farm land, for the Wilson home. The Burnights owned the home until 1957 when it was sold to Robert Smith. In 1977 it was sold to Tom and Robin Hamilton. In 1987, Bruce and Vicky Smith purchased the home.

The "Adams Mansion" about 1926.

Image courtesy of Junette Carter Forsberg.

Current owner Bruce Smith is the great grandson of Milton Smith, the very first owner of all the nearby property. The Smiths have done a marvelous job maintaining the historic integrity of the house. It is a beauty!

Image courtesy of Cristy Clarke Hedgpeth.

OAKDELL

The original owners of this property were the Motts from Des Moines. Exactly when the cottage was built is unknown, but it is listed in the 1906–1907 Lake Region Blue Book. The family did raise the cottage in 1991 to create a better foundation (other than deteriorating tree stumps) and put in a basement. Other improvements have been made to the street side of the cottage. The Pedersen family, and their ancestors, have owned this cottage since 1906.

Oakdell is one of the few cottages that still maintains its original character. This charming, yellow and blue Victorian cottage is possibly the only one on the lake that still has outside stairs from the porch to the upper level bedrooms. This was to avoid getting water and sand in the main living spaces. You would come up from the beach (yes, back in the old days there was a beach here) and go straight to your room to change. The original porch has never been enclosed.

Image courtesy of Cristy Clarke Hedgpeth.

BREEZEWAY

In 1937 Mr. and Mrs. Donald Baxter purchased the cottage from Dr. and Mrs. A. S. Mullin. At that time the front porch was screened with large canvas awnings that would be pulled down on the outside to protect the porch during storms.

Don Baxter was one of the founders of the Okoboji Yacht Club. After races, he would gather young sailors at the cottage to go over who won, who lost, and how to do better next time. Before the current yacht club building was established, many of the yacht club parties were held at the Baxter cottage.

After Baxter's death, daughter, Katherine Everist, took over ownership. Little has changed over the years. The porches are still large but have louvered (jalousie) glass windows to protect them from storms. The swing is still on the side porch, and the family is typically on the front deck watching the sailboat races weekend mornings.

Sadly, Kathy Everist, the "Grand Dame of Okoboji," died in March 2015. Her charming husband preceded her. The cottage has been passed down to their daughters. It is now the summer vacation home of many Baxter/Everist descendants, who will continue the legacy.

Building the Annex to Breezeway.

Image courtesy of the Everist family.

Breezeway, the Everist cottage on Dixon's Beach, a charming, rambling cottage, was built in 1932. It is a replica of Ernest Hemingway's home in Key West. (The resemblance is unmistakable.)

Image courtesy of Kim Everist.

Baxter's daughter, Katherine, held her wedding reception at the cottage and on the grounds. Interestingly, she and her husband, Stephen (Steve) Everist, celebrated not only their fiftieth wedding anniversary at the cottage, but also their sixty-fifth.

Image courtesy of the Everist family.

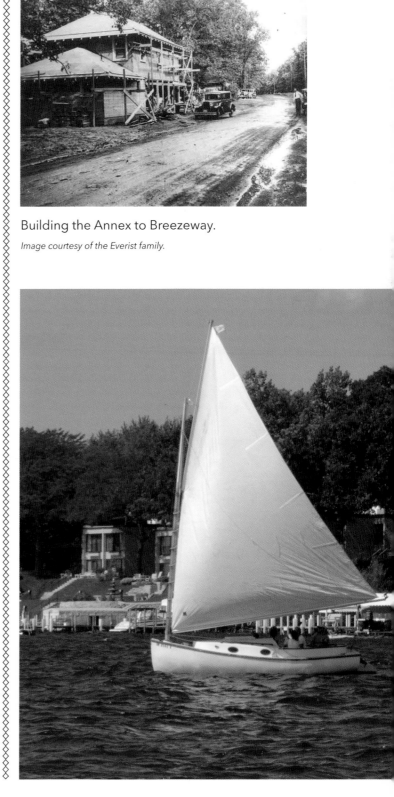

Under Steve and Katherine's tutelage, their children and grandchildren spent their childhoods learning to sail, swimming off the dock, and spending many a summer day at beautiful Lake Okoboji. Their sailboat is one of the last gaff rigged boats on the lake.

Image courtesy of Anne Rehm.

LANDEN HOME

This property traded hands several times. In 1935 the McKee family sold the house to Jules T. Martin. The Martins were in the department store business in Sioux City. No amount of research yielded why the home was built to resemble a ship.

In 1957 the house was sold to Clarence L. Landen of Omaha. The Landens had spent their honeymoon at Okoboji, so to own a piece of lakeshore property was a dream come true.

Over the years changes have been made. The original flat roof was constantly leaking, so a pitched roof was added. The family grew in size and age. With those changes, the need for a master bedroom on ground level was appropriate. Instead of significantly altering the original home, a second residence was built on the property.

The Landen Steamship home, believed to have been built by the Martin family.

Image courtesy of Mary Landen.

The second through fourth generations of the Landen family now enjoy this memorable home.

Image courtesy of Mary Landen.

BRADLEY HOME

In the late 1930s Ed and Mary Delle Bradley, florists from Omaha, built a tiny cottage on a small lot, located midway between Atwell point and Omaha Beach on the steep bank of Echo Bay. In 1953 the original cottage was relocated, and they began the construction of their dream summer lake home.

It was a modern design by an Omaha architect, who was inspired by Ed's admiration of Frank Lloyd Wright's innovative and artistic genius. Designed to integrate into the lake setting, the lower level was set well into the bank, which they dynamited during excavation, causing speculation when construction was begun that some kind of bomb shelter was being built! Actually, it was for the unique dual track boathouse that provides safe and convenient storage for the family's boats.

Above that was built the middle level of the house, a large open room with the lakeside, west facing wall being constructed entirely of glass windows. The outside deck is a favorite spot for entertaining and enjoying breathtaking views of the blue waters of Okoboji. The large open deck on the top level and the lower deck have tubular metal railings that many see as similar to the railings found on a large ship, giving the whole structure a nautical feel, along with the distinctive flag pole/light on the northwest corner.

The living quarters—four bedrooms, bathrooms, kitchen, and living room organized around a central fireplace—are set back from the lake's edge and aren't easily seen from the lake, but are connected by an interior stairwell, also built into the bank. The kitchen area opens into the living area which echoes the open feel of the middle level with a western wall of large glass windows and doors facing out to the lake, a typical softening of the separation between indoors and outdoors seen in much of Wright's architecture.

Over the years few architectural changes have been made, the remaining family honoring the original and well-loved summer home. Current family members all converge at the lake house each summer, for boating, sailing, swimming, sharing memories, and making new ones.

Completed in 1955, the notable Bradley home has captured the interest and admiration of both locals and visitors for many years for its distinctive and nautical architectural design.

Image courtesy of Kelli Farrar.

PEACE HARBOR

Peace Harbor was built in 2004 for Tom and Molly Bedell. Bedell is a well-known and respected name in the lakes area. The family entrepreneurially created their success by initially making fishing lures. This expanded into fishing lines, tow ropes, and just about anything a fisherman would need other than the boat. That company is now known as Pure Fishing.

This home is a work of art. The special places that have been built in are incredible, including spaces like an Irish Pub and large private movie theater. The home has been the host of several fundraisers. With such busy schedules, Tom and Molly have little time to spend in Okoboji. The home, at the time of this publication, is on the market.

Lake view of Peace Harbor in 2015. At just under 25,000 square feet, this is the largest private residence in Iowa.

Image courtesy of Eric Hoien.

EGRALHARVE

These two magnificent old homes are way over one hundred years old. The owners of the homes, according to *Picturesque Souvenir of Spirit Lake and Okoboji Lakes*, in 1896, were Gordon R. Badgerow and J. V. Rider.

The Gordon R. Badgerow family, from Sioux City, named their beach and cottage after their three sons, Egbert, Ralph, and Harve, and thus Egralharve. They purchased the eighty-acre homesteaded farmstead from Rev. Seymour Snyder in 1891. This property runs from Vacation Village/Village West north approximately three fourths of a mile.

At one point, both Badgerow and Rider lived in Dubuque, and it is surmised that this is where they originally met. The Badgerow family seemed to own the vast majority of the property in this area. At one point the ownership of the south home, or the Rider home, went back and forth between Rider and Badgerow.

According to the great grandson of Gordon Badgerow, Thomas Bellaire—and confirmed by the daughter of Frances Ingham, Patty Ingham Davis—at one point the property was used as a resort. Davis still has one of the keys to one of the old "rental" rooms. That door still had the room number on it when they sold the house. She also mentioned that the family was quite certain both houses were Sears Roebuck catalog houses. Bellaire shared that the Badgerows brought in exotic animals (including alligators and peacocks) to entice people to visit and/or stay there. Unfortunately, the animals could not handle the cold, and that effort was dropped after a few years. The "resort" was closed in about 1912.

Two homes built in the 1890s were owned originally by Gordon R. Badgerow and J. V. Rider.

Image courtesy of Iowa Great Lakes Maritime Museum.

Image courtesy of Dickinson County Historical Society & Museum.

Rider cottage, 1896.

Image courtesy of Dickinson County Historical Society & Museum.

Badgerow cottage, 1896.

Not only are there two wonderful old cottages side-by-side, but there is a mineral spring located nearby. Stories suggested that the Indians used to visit this "healing" spring. (Although there are numerous springs in the area, this is the only known mineral spring.) The Badgerow family built a bottling plant in 1912 to capitalize on the spring.

The properties were sold over the years. When looking at the area, you will notice a nice span of grass between the two homes. Frances Hubbell Ingham, from Des Moines, purchased that middle lot for her family. She hired an architect to design a cottage, but the plan was too large for the lot. She approached Joel Herbst, the owner at the time of the Rider home, to see if she could buy an additional five feet of land from him. Instead, he sold her his home. (This was the Rider home.)

Visitors would walk up the stone steps to waiting carriages for the short ride to the mineral fountain/pond for a drink. (Apparently the water tasted just AWFUL.)

Dickinson County Historical Society & Museum.

Patty Ingham Davis reminisced seeing well-dressed women descend from a steamer, which had docked at the property. For several years the venture was very successful. Then came Coca-Cola. The spring is still there off in the grasses, and if you go scuba diving, you might find a Badgerow bottle.

Image courtesy of Thomas Bellaire.

Hubby, and his wife, Kathy, did extensive remodeling of the old Badgerow home. It is still owned by the Inghams.

Image courtesy of Steve Christensen.

In 2014 Patty and her husband decided they didn't need so much space. They sold the south home (Rider home) to Steve Christensen.

Image courtesy of Steve Christensen.

Later, the home to the north (Badgerow home) became available, and Frances purchased it as well. She liked the idea of a compound for the family. Frances and two of her children, Hubbell "Hubby" and Patty, moved to the Badgerow home, and named it "Toad Hall." (It had been known as the "Big House" during the Badgerows' ownership.) The south home became a guest house for the rest of the Ingham family. The kids named it "Versailles." Upon Frances's death, Hubby took possession of the north home and Patty the south home.

FREDORA

According to the Dickinson County Assessor's website, the Fredora cottage was built in 1890. What draws most people's attention to the property is the seawall with the name "FREDORA" painted on it. The Dickinson County Auditor's office was most helpful and explained just who Fred and Dora were.

Fred and Dora Smith came from La Crosse, Wisconsin. They bought the property on Manhattan Beach in 1901. In 1910 Dora dedicated a strip of land to the public. At some point they painted "FREDORA" on their seawall. The Smiths sold the cottage to Mr. and Mrs. George Carpenter. Mrs. Carpenter promised her husband she would never ask for anything again if he bought her the cottage. Sadly, it wasn't too long before she died. The cottage later became the property of their daughter, Isabelle Carpenter. She owned it until the early 1990s.

Gayle and T. J. Reardon from Sioux Falls, South Dakota, were vacationing on Omaha Beach in the summer of 1991. While on a tandem bicycle ride, they ran into a realtor who told them about a wonderful fixer-upper on Manhattan Beach. Later that day they visited the house.

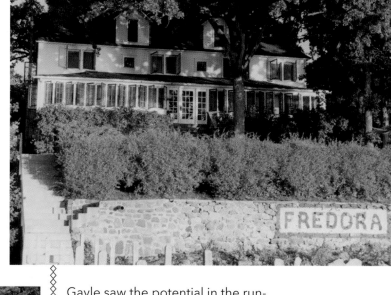

Gayle saw the potential in the run-down residence, and thus began the "love affair" between the Reardons and Fredora.

Image courtesy of T. J. Reardon.

Fredora after a lot of TLC by the Reardons.

Image courtesy of T. J. Reardon.

THE PEACOCK & MURIEL TURNLEY

Less about two buildings and more about a colorful woman, is this gem of the lake. Muriel Window was born in 1895 in a small town in Kansas. She began performing at a young age and moved to New York City where she performed at the Met, the American Music Hall, and the Ziegfeld Follies. Old-timers might remember Muriel cigars—yup, for Muriel Turnley.

She was married three times. Her third husband, Howard Turnley, brought her to Arnolds Park in the 1930s. She called herself "The Lady of the Lake."

Howard Turnley died in 1946, but Muriel kept the businesses going. Liquor laws were not appreciated by Muriel, and she didn't always observe their closing hours. She put up with "getting busted" for a while, but when the fourth time came one year, Muriel closed up shop and moved to Lauderdale-by-the-Sea, Florida, and opened the Jade House. Muriel died in 1971.

Menu from The Peacock.

Image courtesy of Don McCulloch.

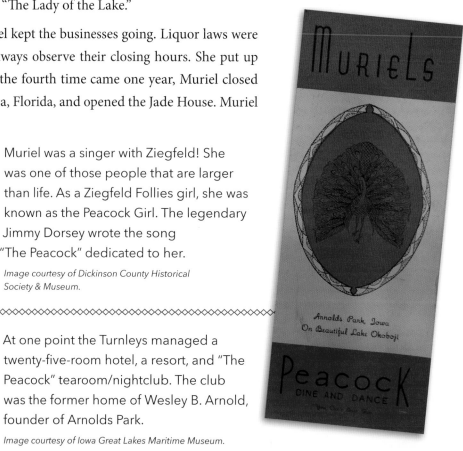

Muriel was a singer with Ziegfeld! She was one of those people that are larger than life. As a Ziegfeld Follies girl, she was known as the Peacock Girl. The legendary Jimmy Dorsey wrote the song "The Peacock" dedicated to her.

Image courtesy of Dickinson County Historical Society & Museum.

At one point the Turnleys managed a twenty-five-room hotel, a resort, and "The Peacock" tearoom/nightclub. The club was the former home of Wesley B. Arnold, founder of Arnolds Park.

Image courtesy of Iowa Great Lakes Maritime Museum.

Muriel (left) and her bookkeeper, Arlene O'Farrell, were on holiday at Club 21 in NYC. (Photographs of Muriel are rare.)

Image courtesy of O'Farrell family.

For a feel of The Peacock, visit the Okoboji Classic Car Museum. A full-size replica of her nightclub has been recreated there.

Image courtesy of Cristy Clarke Hedgpeth.

Inside the great room is a catwalk elevated about twelve feet. This was Muriel's "stage." She would have friends over, disappear, and come out of a small room clad in amazing costumes, singing. She would then descend the circular stairs to join her friends.

Image courtesy of Okoboji Magazine.

Muriel's home was on the lake a short distance from the nightclub. Near the door off the street is embedded a six-foot-wide star cast in the concrete. That is because Muriel was the star!

Julie Fillenwarth purchased the cottage in 1984 and has done a great job retaining its historic features. Julie was quoted saying, "She was one of the all-time great characters around here."

Image courtesy of Okoboji Magazine.

CAMPS

Gather round the campfire, bring your sleeping bag, and hear the stories of some of the camps at Lake Okoboji. Since the early 1900s there have been organized camps at the lakes. Most were faith-based.

CAMP FOSTER

When thinking of camps in the lakes region, Camp Foster comes to mind. Although it is not on West Okoboji, it needs to be included in this book. Current executive director, Josh Carr, shared the story.

Being the oldest YMCA camp in Iowa, and one of the oldest in the United States, Camp Foster YMCA has many wonderful, rich traditions. Those who have had the chance to experience the "magic" of the "Foster Flame" can relate that Camp Foster has many unique qualities.

Image courtesy of Camp Foster.

In 1912, the dream of State Boys' Work Secretary, Leonard Paulson, began to take form. On the south shore of East Lake Okoboji, land to be used for the State YMCA camp was purchased for $5,000. Among the purchasers were Thomas D. Foster, Charles and Clyde Brenton, J. H. Allen, and H. C. Wallace. The original forty-seven acres were adjacent to the location of the Howe family cabin (Spirit Lake Massacre). Camp Foster has since grown to 214 acres, which includes that point of historic interest.

For the first couple of decades, a road to the camp was not available, so campers and staff would arrive by steamer originating in Arnold's Park and would pass through the swing bridge onto East Lake.

Image courtesy of Iowa Great Lakes Maritime Museum.

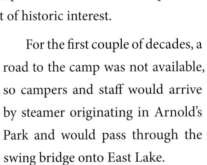

During the first years, Camp Foster was a boys-only camp, coined "State Camp for Boys." This 1912 image shows the camp tents and a friendly game of volleyball.

The faculty (1912). Button-up shirts and ties seemed the norm.
Image courtesy of Camp Foster.

Jim Fisher photo = Original scans provided

Image courtesy of Camp Foster.

In the early days (1917), Camp Foster's primary waterfront programs were swimming, fishing, boating, and athletics, supplemented with singing and devotional bible study.

Jim Fisher photo = Original scans provided @ 120(

The cook tent (1912).
Image courtesy of Camp Foster.

Other than some "day-only" camps in the 1920s, girls did not begin attending camp until the 1930s, and the sessions were not coed. The first coed session was offered in the summer of 1970. The idea came from parents who requested that both their sons and daughters could attend camp the same week to reduce transportation costs. (Photo circa 1960s.)

Image courtesy of Camp Foster.

The motto of the camp was, "Each for all and all for each." Part of the big component of Camp Foster "magic" is the way kids feel when they attend camp.

Today, many of the programs are the same or similar to those in years past. In addition to the lakefront activities, classic camp activities include crafts, archery, marksmanship, ropes-challenge course, equestrian programs, nature programs, as well as leadership training. The importance of the YMCA mission, "To put Christian principles into practice through programs that build healthy spirit, mind and body for all," is just as important today as they were in the days of the steamers.

Because of the practice of this mission, children feel very much a part of something special and make lasting friendships and memories. For decades, another of the camp's big programs has been day camp. The day camp has undergone a number of models and even names throughout the years, but the mission and focus on kids has remained the same.

The real "magic" of Camp Foster comes from blessings passed down from the forefathers and the legacy that embraces valuing every child and teaching them the values of respect, honesty, responsibility, caring, and fairness. The natural resources of the lakes area have helped children connect with the peaceful nature of being outdoors in the summertime.

Camp Foster celebrates a diverse population that includes many children who, without financial assistance, would not have the means to attend camp. The YMCA's scholarship programs have been a huge part of this and have been steadily growing in recent years thanks to many generous contributors.

Image courtesy of Camp Foster.

Camp Foster has had many amazing opportunities to work with community organizations from across the country. This list includes churches, schools, Boys and Girls Clubs, universities, businesses, and service clubs. Some of the recently notable partnerships include National TTT Society, American Lung Association/Sanford Hospitals, United States Military Kids, and Miracle Burn Camp, which celebrated twenty years in 2015. Camp Foster hosts the only integrated camp for burn survivors in the United States.

Today, children from coast to coast, and from across the oceans, travel to Camp Foster to have that feeling of belonging and freedom from the constraints of their hometown environment.

Image courtesy of Camp Foster.

LAKE OKOBOJI UNITED METHODIST CAMP

In 1915, the camp property was recommended for purchase by a commission from the Sheldon District of the United Methodist Church. The purchase price was $15,000. At the time of purchase, the site was less than a mile from the popular West Okoboji station of the Rock Island Railroad, and two and half miles directly west of Spirit Lake.

Since those early years more than a hundred years ago, the ministry at Okoboji has changed hearts and lives. All camping events encourage campers to learn, play, experience God's love in the outdoors, grow in faith in a safe atmosphere, and to reach their personal best, according to Bryan Johnson, site director of the Lake Okoboji United Methodist Camp.

Campers and guests enjoy wonderful food service, air-conditioned/heated facilities, cutting edge programming, the opportunity to grow in faith & leadership, and warm Christian hospitality from trained staff.

Just off the shores of West Lake Okoboji lies over a hundred beautiful acres of camp, conference, and retreat opportunities in the heart of the Iowa Great Lakes.

Image courtesy of Lake Okoboji United Methodist Camp.

The first building on camp property was the Tabernacle (pictured below in about 1920), constructed as a gathering area for the popular northwest Iowa camp meeting that eventually became the Northwest Iowa Bible Conference. On September 30, 1926, the Tabernacle was demolished by a tornado.

In 1927, a new brick building was constructed on the Tabernacle grounds at a cost of $8,000, just in time for that year's camp meeting. In 2012, a decommissioning service was held on camp property to celebrate the life of the tabernacle building.

Image courtesy of Mary Schiltz Jensen.

Image courtesy of Lake Okoboji United Methodist Camp.

In 1991, the Iowa Annual Conference of the United Methodist Church purchased ninety-four acres of farmland adjacent to the existing camp. This farmland, now known as the South Campus, has been developed for camping and retreat ministries.

Today, the Lake Okoboji United Methodist Camp provides a dynamic, ACA-accredited camping program throughout the summer and comfortable retreat space during the non-summer seasons.

Camping at the Lake Okoboji United Methodist Camp has been a life-changing experience for over a hundred years. In addition to both classic and modern programming such as archery, canoeing, mountain boards, go-karts, climbing, and crafts, all participants make new friends and experience God's love in new and exciting ways.

Images courtesy of Lake Okoboji United Methodist Camp.

YWCA/WALTHER LEAGUE/CAMP OKOBOJI

The Young Women's Christian Association (YWCA) purchased twenty-seven acres of land in Emerson Bay in 1919 to provide a vacation camp for industrious women. Five former Army barracks were brought in for housing. In the summer of 1920, its first year with campers, the YWCA was filled to its capacity of 235.

Over the years, the YWCA purchased additional land and replaced the barracks with cottages. A spacious dining hall and recreational facilities were also added. Besides groups of women, the camp was later opened to other conference groups but then sat vacant for a few years until purchased by the Walther League in 1940.

Aerial view of the YWCA campground (1921).

Image courtesy of Luckybreak/Okoboji.

The Lodge at the Walther League.

Image courtesy of Iowa Great Lakes Maritime Museum.

The Pergola at the YWCA camp (circa 1920s).

Image courtesy of Iowa Great Lakes Maritime Museum.

In 1940 the Iowa West Walther League purchased the property and on May 31, 1940, reopened for the first annual Walther League three-day conference. Thousands were in attendance. Cottages were remodeled, and some were now available for family use. The facility was opened to other organizations as well as Lutherans.

Image courtesy of Luckybreak/Okoboji.

Camp Okoboji was formerly known as the Walther League Camp until the late 1960s, according to current executive director, Doug Kading. The camp celebrated seventy-five years of Outdoor Ministry in 2015.

The Walther League Camp name was changed to Camp Okoboji when the league of young men and women who made up the Walther League dissolved and the camp needed its own identity. Beginning about 1960, the once "summer only" camp began the transition to a year-round facility. By 1989 winter lodging was available for up to a hundred people. Today winter lodging is available for three hundred guests.

Camp Okoboji is a Recognized Service Organization of the Lutheran Church–Missouri Synod and is owned by all the members of the congregations in the western half of Iowa. It continues to provide ministry to children in kindergarten through sixth grade as well as junior and senior high youth, families, and adults.

Education and training in God's Word, recreation, sports, the arts, crafts, and spending quality time with family and friends are some of the many activities which take place in this unique and beautiful setting.

Image courtesy of Camp Okoboji.

With the assistance of Laborers for Christ (retired men and women who find a purpose in serving their Lord and their fellow man by remodeling existing facilities and constructing new), Camp Okoboji has constructed a climate-controlled addition on Bats Roost (renamed the Bethel Retreat Center) that lodges up to ninety-two.

Image courtesy of Camp Okoboji.

The camp's mission is to bring people of all ages together to be with "Jesus at the Lake" while enjoying His creation of water, air, and soil.

Image courtesy of Camp Okoboji.

They also constructed a new maintenance building, a year-round family lodging unit and dormitory, and a small white framed chapel called The Refuge.

FLOETE MANSION/OKOBOJI CLUB/LAKESHORE CENTER

This property, situated along the west shore of Miller's Bay, has the most amazing history of transformations. In 1917 Franklin Floete, a Spencer, Iowa lumberman, built this $135,000 mansion on 650 feet of lakefront property on a seventy-acre tract.

Other support buildings were on the grounds, including a carriage house and an ice storage building. The Floetes lived there in lavish lifestyle for only a few years. Franklin died and his wife left for a home in California and never returned.

In 1927 the home was offered to President Calvin Coolidge as a summer White House. Instead, Coolidge spent his summer in the Black Hills, South Dakota.

In 1942 there was a small fire in the roof. The structure was repaired and back on the market. A small group of investors purchased the property in 1945 and turned it into a private club called the Okoboji Club.

Lester Heinsheimer, from Sioux Falls, became the sole owner when the Okoboji Club opened in May 1946. Small cottages were built on the property for members to use from May 1 to late October.

Image courtesy of Iowa Great Lakes Maritime Museum.

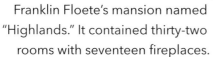

Grand entryway and stairs at the Okoboji Club.

Image courtesy of Lakeshore Center at Okoboji.

Franklin Floete's mansion named "Highlands." It contained thirty-two rooms with seventeen fireplaces.

Image courtesy of Luckybreak/Okoboji.

Image courtesy of Lakeshore Center at Okoboji.

A devastating fire totally destroyed the building on April 14, 1951.

One of the three dining rooms available at the Okoboji Club (circa 1946).

Image courtesy of Luckybreak/Okoboji.

Current executive director, Beth Ehlers, shared many amazing photographs and stories and brought the story up-to-date. In 1954, some forward-thinking men and women on behalf of area Presbyteries decided to purchase the property that had been known as the Okoboji Club. Out of the ashes, the Presbyterian camp on Okoboji was created. The first summer camping season was held in 1956 and has continued ever since.

Girls in one of the cabins circa 1960.

Peaceful time in the shade of the cabins (background), which were added during the Okoboji Club days.

Images courtesy of Lakeshore Center at Okoboji.

The ice house from the Floete mansion days was repurposed twice for the camp.

The base of one of the many fireplaces from the original mansion is currently used as a grill.

Image courtesy of Lakeshore Center at Okoboji.

In 2009, the Lodge was completed and opened, allowing for more comfortable accommodations for adults. This also allowed for year-round programming.

Image courtesy of Lakeshore Center at Okoboji.

In 2014, the name was changed to Lakeshore Center at Okoboji to make it more welcoming and inviting to groups that are not Presbyterian. This has provided a center for many to be able to retreat in the beauty of God's creation and reconnect with their faith, their families, and just to gain new perspectives on life. Lakeshore has become a comfortable oasis from the busyness of daily life for many.

Lakeshore Center has hosted many church gatherings, business meetings, and educational opportunities over the past sixty years. It is an ideal location for family gatherings, reunions, weddings, and, of course, summer camp for all ages.

Guests of Lakeshore Center can enjoy peaceful walks along nature trails, canoeing and kayaking, swimming in beautiful West Lake Okoboji, and, with the help of trained staff, take on the challenges of low and high ropes courses. There is a labyrinth, archery field, and lots of campfire rings to enjoy a roaring campfire and everyone's favorite, s'mores.

Image courtesy of Lakeshore Center at Okoboji.

Lakeshore Center at Okoboji has had an important effect on many lives, as thousands of campers and guests have come for spiritual and physical refreshment, learning and developing new skills and fresh insights. This secluded setting is located on fifty-five acres along the shores of West Lake Okoboji, with 600 feet of beautiful sand beach, complete with a canopy of large oak trees.

CASINO/LA SALLETTE SEMINARY/BOYS TOWN

The south end of Brown's Bay was once a desolate sand bank. It lacked any charm. But this area became one of the largest landscape projects in Iowa.

In the summer of 1892, Dr. H. O. Green of Spencer took a buggy ride with Msgr. P. F. McGrath and the Rev. Fr. J. L. Kirby out to see West Okoboji. The Monsignor declared his desire to spend his aging years on the lake. Dr. Green then heard of a tract of land that had become available. The property was originally land destined for a narrow-gage railroad, but that never came to be and was eventually for sale. Monsignor McGrath said he would buy the land if Dr. Green went in as a full partner. The total price for the 160 acres was $8,000.

Msgr. McGrath suggested the land be developed into residential lots. (All that was there was a narrow strip of sand.) Dr. Green then hired not one, but two different landscape architects to look at the property. Both architects declared the property a gem and work began almost immediately. Surveys were taken over the winter.

The large second level was a spacious dance hall with large porches overlooking the lake. The Casino was a popular destination. Historian Aubrey LaFoy fondly remembered going there as a child to watch the activity held on the grounds. In the early 1930s there were dancers, singers, skaters, dog shows, acrobats—you name it!

Image courtesy of Iowa Great Lakes Maritime Museum.

The two-story Casino had a steel structure and was made of brick with a stucco finish. The lower level contained a bath house, soda fountain, dining area, and other spaces—but no acknowledged gambling.

Image courtesy of Iowa Great Lakes Maritime Museum.

Monsignor McGrath was traveling at this time in Italy and became ill and died. Meanwhile, Dr. Green had started work on the roads (which were all curved to allow each property to have a view). As the entire project was now in the hands and purse strings of Dr. Green, he began to do a lot of the work himself. All 6,000 of the trees and shrubs were planted by Green. This area was named Terrace Park and opened to the public in 1905.

In 1923 Dr. and Mrs. Green built the Casino. This was the same year the Central Ballroom opened in Arnold's Park.

In the afternoon of April 30, 1936, a strong tornado wreaked havoc on Terrace Park. The Casino itself was hardly damaged, but the Green's home and nearly everything else around was destroyed. The Casino reopened, but soon closed and remained closed for several years. The Greens lost heart and the area became desolate.

Once again a tornado plagued the property. There were sixty boys huddled in the basement when the tornado of 1968 hit the beach. Although there was damage, no one was hurt.

Today Boys Town remains the owner of this magnificent stretch of beach. There are now boys and girls in attendance. The students must earn the right to come to the lake from the original Father Flanagan's Boys' Home located in Omaha.

TERRACE PARK ON WEST OKOBOJI LAKE

In 1940 the property was ceded to the Catholic Church. The Lady of the Lake camp was established, and a seminary for the order of LaSalette took over. The once open porches on the second story were enclosed. This was only a temporary location for LaSalette, whose former location back East had burned but was now rebuilt.

Image courtesy of Luckybreak/Okoboji.

In the summer of 1953, Boys Town, a special home and school for wayward boys and young men based in Omaha, took over the facility. There would be seventy to a hundred boys visiting every week. In 1961 the old building was torn down and a new one erected that functioned better for the summer of 1962.

Image courtesy of Mary Schiltz Jensen.

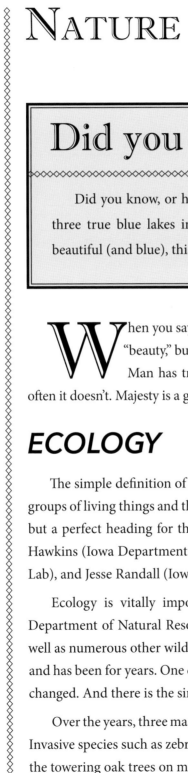

NATURE

Did you know?

Did you know, or hear, that according to *National Geographic*, Okoboji is one of just three true blue lakes in the world. Although most would agree the lake is stunningly beautiful (and blue), this statement is not true, just urban legend.

When you say the word nature, many images come to mind. First is probably "beauty," but then you think of the storms and tremendous power they hold. Man has tried to control or manipulate nature. Sometimes it works, but often it doesn't. Majesty is a good word for this incredible place on our earth called Okoboji.

ECOLOGY

The simple definition of ecology is "a science that deals with the relationships between groups of living things and their environments." This became quite a buzzword in the 1960s, but a perfect heading for this information provided with the help of professionals, Mike Hawkins (Iowa Department of Natural Resources, the DNR), Jane Shuttleworth (Lakeside Lab), and Jesse Randall (Iowa State University Forestry).

Ecology is vitally important relative to the history and future of the lakes. The Department of Natural Resources (DNR) oversees the Lake Patrol and Fish Hatchery, as well as numerous other wildlife issues. Lakeside Lab is tremendously important to the lake and has been for years. One can't write a story of the lake without including how fishing has changed. And there is the simple fact that the water levels change.

Over the years, three massive dredging projects helped create new waterfront properties. Invasive species such as zebra mussels is a relatively new concern, as is oak wilt threatening the towering oak trees on many properties ringing the lake.

WATERSHED

The Iowa Great Lakes chain, like most other lake systems, is fed by the land draining to it—the watershed. Water falling on the land can reach the lake fairly quickly by stream, or runoff, and can also soak into the ground and move more slowly as groundwater.

Conservation efforts in the watershed have targeted over 1,300 acres of wetland restoration since 1980. Because of the influence of a watershed on lake water quality, conservation efforts in residential and agricultural areas are a focus of today's efforts to protect these resources. Wetlands play a key role in slowing water in the watershed and filtering out pollutants.

Iowa Great Lakes Watershed

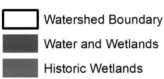

☐ Watershed Boundary

⬛ Water and Wetlands

⬛ Historic Wetlands

Dickinson County, IA

The Iowa Great Lakes watershed contains 85,933 acres of land and lakes stretching all the way into Minnesota and ending just south of Interstate 90. In Minnesota, Loon Lake, Pearl Lake, Little Spirit Lake, and Clear Lake are all part of the chain. Prior to European settlement, it is estimated that 37% or 32,400 acres of the watershed was water (lakes and wetlands). By 1980, over 45% (14,400 acres) of the wetlands in the watershed had been drained.

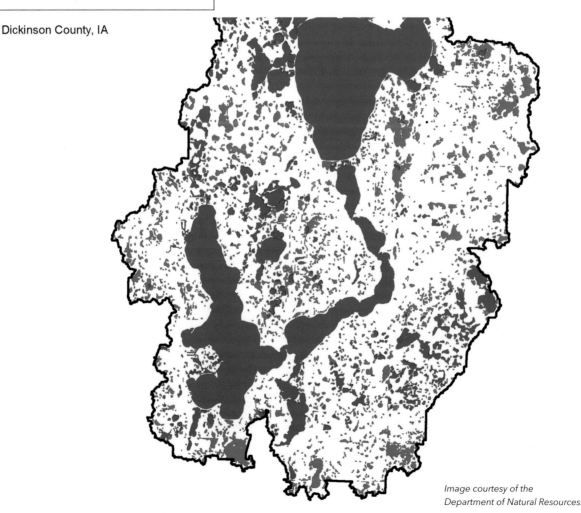

Image courtesy of the
Department of Natural Resources.

Did you know?

The lake "flips" twice a year! Here's how and why:

The surface and bottom waters of all lakes mix, but West Okoboji—compared to other glacial lakes in Iowa—is unique because the surface and bottom waters mix only twice a year, making it a dimictic (twice mixing) lake. The unusual depth of West Okoboji at over 136 feet at its deepest spot compared to other lakes in Iowa is what makes it dimictic. While shallow lakes can mix—or in layman's terms flip or turn over on a daily basis—West Okoboji is so deep that the top and bottom layers only mix when the water temperature is relatively constant from top to bottom, and these conditions occur only in the spring and fall.

During the summer when days are long and the air is warm, the lake surface heats faster than the water underneath. Cold water is denser than warm water and sinks to the bottom of the lake. Usually by the end of May, a stable layer of warm surface water forms on West Okoboji, overlying a layer of cold, deep water. In shallow lake systems, these layers mix when the wind blows and re-form on a sunny, still day, but not in deep lakes like Okoboji. The upper warm layer is about thirty feet deep and stays stable all summer long no matter how hard the wind blows until fall arrives.

Then, shorter days and dropping temperatures cause the surface water to cool and become denser. The denser water sinks, replacing and mixing with the underlying water, which mixes its way up to the surface in what is popularly called turnover. From fall through winter, water temperatures stay fairly uniform under the ice—just under freezing. When spring arrives, however, the melting ice cools the surface water, making it denser, and once again causing it to sink and mix with the bottom water up to the surface.

Each time this happens, the bottom waters bring organic material to the surface, in a sense fertilizing the lake and providing nutrients to start a new cycle of aquatic life. Thanks to Jane Shuttleworth, Lakeside Labs, for the explanation.

This is the reason cold-water fish, like trout, won't survive the summer in the lake. The top layer of warm water is the only place with enough oxygen, but it's too warm for trout.

P.S.: And when the lake "flips," your boat won't flip with it.

The Lakeside Lab GLEON research buoy, installed in 2015, collects weather and water quality data simultaneously every ten minutes. It also includes a string of sensors in six-foot intervals from the surface to the bottom of the lake, allowing for the first time detailed measurements of fall turnover.

Images courtesy of Lakeside Lab.

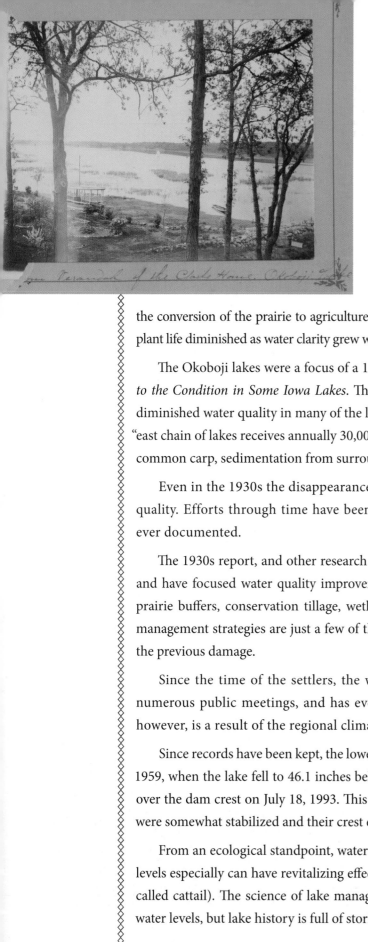

Historically, aquatic plant life in these lakes was much more abundant and diverse. The earliest accounts in the late 1800s of the lakes area noted the clear water of the Okoboji lakes with numerous aquatic plants and rushes.

Image courtesy of Iowa Great Lakes Maritime Museum.

As the towns and developments of the area grew, sewage and waste disposal became an issue. Along with wetland drainage and the conversion of the prairie to agriculture and towns, the lake water quality was dramatically altered. Aquatic plant life diminished as water clarity grew worse.

The Okoboji lakes were a focus of a 1930s *Report to the Iowa State Fish and Game Department Relative to the Condition in Some Iowa Lakes.* This study outlined the causes of "objectionable algae" blooms and diminished water quality in many of the lakes in the Iowa Great Lakes chain. This report estimated that the "east chain of lakes receives annually 30,000,000 gallons of sewage water." This report also identified invasive common carp, sedimentation from surrounding shorelines, and agricultural fields as additional influences.

Even in the 1930s the disappearance of aquatic plants was identified as a contributor to poor water quality. Efforts through time have been made to replant some of these species, but little success was ever documented.

The 1930s report, and other research conducted since, confirmed the factors influencing water quality and have focused water quality improvement and protection efforts seen today. Rain gardens, bioswales, prairie buffers, conservation tillage, wetland restorations, sanitary sewage treatment, and common carp management strategies are just a few of the tools used today to protect the lakes and even reverse some of the previous damage.

Since the time of the settlers, the water level in the lakes has been a subject of local discussion, numerous public meetings, and has even been discussed in the State Capital. Most of this variation, however, is a result of the regional climate and local weather events.

Since records have been kept, the lowest lake level recorded on West Lake Okoboji was on September 20, 1959, when the lake fell to 46.1 inches below the dam crest. On the other extreme, the lake hit 55.4 inches over the dam crest on July 18, 1993. This is nearly an 8.5-foot swing in water levels. The levels in the lakes were somewhat stabilized and their crest elevation permanently set with the addition of dams.

From an ecological standpoint, water level fluctuations are an important part of lake health. Low water levels especially can have revitalizing effects for many important species of water plants like bulrush (often called cattail). The science of lake management today recognizes some of the past misconceptions about water levels, but lake history is full of stories related to dams, floods, and droughts.

In the latter part of the 1800s, a mill was located at the isthmus on East Okoboji called the Old Red Mill. (Lore does not tell what kind of mill this was.) In 1870 Mr. Stimpson sold this mill to O. Compton. Compton updated the mill with a much larger wheel that needed a steady flow of water to properly run.

In 1869, Mr. A. D. Foster from Wisconsin built a sawmill, and the first grist mill, at the base of Lower Gar. In the 1800s Iowa was well known for its wheat crop. The grist mill was needed to efficiently process wheat. This mill was highly popular, and farmers from miles around would line up to use it. When the grist mill and adjoining dam were built, the water levels were low, so building the dam and mill was easy. However, when the water level declined, the Compton mill, up north, did not operate well.

A group of Compton's friends got together to demolish the lower dam. Foster immediately made repairs to his dam. Compton's friends returned to do a better job tearing it up. After tiring of fighting this "dam" issue, Compton gave up, realizing his mill would never be a success owing to low water levels. If it wasn't one extreme, it was another. Residents then complained about how high the water was due to the Foster dam. However, a drought was on its way. By 1886 the water was so low he had to put in steam power to run his mill.

According to the 1881–1882 State Fish Commission biennial report, the state was petitioned to install an "obstruction or fish-rack" as the existing dam was not permitting the fish to return to the lakes during spawning season. In the 1892–1893 report there was a recommendation for a dam with a fish weir to keep the fish in the lakes. In 1896 a stone and cement dam was built. This one had a system of screens to allow the water to pass but restrain the passage of fish. By 1907–1908 the water was once again at a high level and the state took out the dam. Another dam was built in 1911. It was later replaced in 1919.

The current concrete dam (with the recent addition of the electric fish barrier) was constructed in 1971 and 1972. This dam was built to the same level as the old one just a few yards downstream. Remnants (stone, concrete, and wood pilings) of the old dam can still be seen just downstream of the new dam.

In 1911 this dam was built at the bottom of Lower Gar in conjunction with the Okoboji Protective Association. It was built of boulders, cobbles, and wooden planks.

Image courtesy of the Department of Natural Resources

AQUATIC INVASIVE SPECIES

Today, ecological threats to the lakes continue. Aquatic invasive species seem to be of increasing importance. The early introductions of common carp were followed with other unintended introductions of nonnative species such as yellow bass, first discovered in 2005.

In 2011, bighead carp and the jumping silver carp entered the lakes during a high water event that flooded the Little Sioux and Missouri Rivers. These fish traveled over 200 miles from the Missouri River up the Little Sioux to get here. This species won't reproduce in the lakes. However, the community quickly organized an effort to block future migrations from downstream in an effort to keep their numbers low.

In 2012, the first three zebra mussels were discovered in East Lake Okoboji and Upper Gar. Today, this species has spread to the entire chain. Every fall, when the boat hoists are removed, the DNR would look for mussel shells clinging to the structures. In 2013 their numbers increased, and in 2014 they were widespread but low in numbers. That all changed in the fall of 2015. They had exponentially spread.

What does this mean for the lakes? According to Mike Hawkins of the DNR/Fish Hatchery, we will probably see several changes. First, swimmers are urged to wear foot protection as the shells can be quite sharp. Visitors and residents will probably see increased clarity to the water because the mussels are filter feeders and in large numbers can filter vast volumes of lake water.

A new electric fish barrier was added at a cost of $1,038,000 to the bottom of the dam to stop additional invasive fish, like the Asian jumping carp, during flooding times. (Funds came from many organizations as well as the state of Minnesota.) Higher wing walls were also built to help contain flood waters. This project was accomplished in short order. The initial request for information was on April 9, 2012. That request went to design and engineering, was then sent for bids in October 2012, and because of perfect weather and low water levels, the work was completed quickly. On February 5, 2013, the barrier was operational. (The electrical component only comes into play when the water is flowing over the dam.)

Image courtesy of the Department of Natural Resources.

The bottom of ladder rungs at the end of the 2015 season covered with zebra mussels.

Images courtesy of Jim Hedgpeth.

That increase in water clarity will lead to a couple of changes. Aquatic plants will have more light available for growth, and some native juvenile fish will likely have less plankton to feed on. The drinking water utilities that pull water from West Lake Okoboji have already had to make big changes to their intake systems to prevent the mussels from plugging them. The Spirit Lake Hatchery has engineering under way to do the same. If fewer walleyes can survive as tiny fry because of lower plankton levels, then the hatchery will be faced with finding ways to raise larger, more expensive fingerlings.

There is talk about a method to eradicate the mussels. It is quite costly, but hopefully this will become a nonissue in the future.

Lake watchers are on the lookout for other potentially invasive species. Eurasian watermilfoil, brittle naiad, spiny waterflea, and hydrilla are just a few of the other aquatic invaders making their way across the country. These plants and animals have the ability to grow and expand like crazy, with few natural predators or natural diseases to keep them in check. The only way to slow down this spread is for all boaters to clean, drain, and dry their boats and trailers before moving from one lake or river to the next.

FORESTRY

Not all invasive species are water related. In recent years many of the beautiful oak trees that surround the lake have become infected with oak wilt or bur oak blight. Dr. Jesse Randall, ISU Extension Forester, explained what is going on.

Sadly, oak wilt is transferred in two manners. A sick tree can infect a healthy oak through below-ground transmission when two of the same species of oak form root grafts. The other method occurs after a tree has been pruned during the summer months when the primary insect vector flies from oak wilt spore mats growing on infected trees and lands on the freshly opened pruning wound. (So only prune in the dead of winter.)

Of the three varieties of oaks in the lakes region, red oaks are especially susceptible and can be killed three to six weeks after being infected. It can take white and bur oaks years to succumb, and normally death occurs after a secondary stress, like drought, occurs.

Bur oak blight is a different problem. This is a native pathogen that creates a lesion in the leaf vein. This kills the leaf but also tricks the tree into not shedding that leaf petiole. With the petiole attached, the new buds that grow into new stems and leaves the following year are infected with the pathogen. After several years the tree is weakened and becomes susceptible to other problems such as oak wilt and two-lined chestnut borer.

The good news about bur oak blight is that it does not appear to be transferred tree to tree via root grafts but can and is moved by rain splash.

Then there is the Emerald Ash Bore. The larvae of this insect will burrow into the ash tree and during their development period eat the vascular structure of the tree causing the tree to "self-desiccate" and die. Although the insect can fly over a mile, the vast majority choose to return to the original tree or a close neighboring ash tree. Most new infestations have been spread inadvertently by man.

Through the movement of firewood, the bug in its hidden larval stage can be moved into new areas. This can be held in check by not transporting in firewood, through chemical or heat treatment of firewood that is to be moved, and through chemical treatments of living trees in infested areas.

Evidence of lethal oak wilt is obvious in winter, as leaves remain on infected trees.

Image courtesy of Craig Wilson, certified arborist.

Another invasive problem is the Emerald Ash Borer. This is a relatively small insect that came from Asia. The lake's ash trees have no immunity to the ash borer.

Images courtesy of the USDA.

So the long and short is that the region may lose a good number of trees. Most of the trees surrounding the lake are quite old. The older a tree, the more susceptible it is to problems. Dr. Randall recommended planting an assortment of trees, such as maple and hickory. Diversity is the ideal way to minimize risk from pests and pathogens that continue to arrive on the lakeshore. Promising research results from ISU show trees originating from big bur oak acorns are much more blight resistant (but their acorns are golf-ball size). Time to start planting.

All of these invasive species can create havoc with the native ecosystem. Most of their impacts are hard to predict and are yet to be realized. The Iowa Great Lakes community has not only rallied to construct infrastructure like the electric fish barrier, but has also focused effort and funding toward partnering with the Iowa DNR and Lakeside Laboratory to put college interns at area boat ramps to inspect boats and trailers and educate boaters about the threats of aquatic invasive species. This program has reached tens of thousands of boaters.

FISHING

The lakes have long been an angler's paradise, whether fishing from the shore, dropping a line off the dock, or casting from a fishing boat. The "lure" of lake fishing keeps local bait shops thriving and fish stories in abundance.

In the 1870s, common, or German, carp were introduced into Iowa as a highly prized food source and sport fish. If only they had known the future impact of that decision. As water quality and habitat declined, so did the fishing. Unregulated fishing also added to the problem.

In the early days, some gamefish were transported from the backwaters of the Mississippi. Included were small paddlefish, commonly called spoonbills. Paddlefish may have also migrated up the Little Sioux River from their native habitat in the Missouri River. These fish would grow to more than a hundred pounds. The largest caught in West Lake Okoboji weighed 210 pounds in 1916. Paddlefish are prehistoric in appearance and have cartilage, instead of bones, like a shark. They use their huge mouths to filter plankton and have no teeth. Paddlefish have long since disappeared since their spawning activity only occurs in rivers.

Four locals (left to right) Bert O'Farrell, Guy Rickman, Harry Tennant, and Kit Wilcox each nabbed one spoonbill ice fishing.

Image courtesy of Martha Green.

Image courtesy of Doyne Wilson Hummel and Dickinson County News.

Quite the catch in 1894.

Fishing has changed dramatically at the lakes over the years. Even in the mid to late 1800s, fishing was a major attraction to the lakes. Anglers would go out in their boats and come back to empty out their boats of all the fish they had caught. Often so many were caught they were thrown into the fields as fertilizer.

Image courtesy of Martha Green.

A fish hatchery was constructed in 1880 between Big Spirit Lake and East Lake Okoboji to raise additional fish for stocking (across the road from the Hotel Orleans). During the first year, 200,000 Lake Superior trout eggs and 500,000 white fish eggs were hatched. The hatchery also experimented with walleye, black crappie, buffalo, and yellow perch during its first years. Mallard ducks were also hatched for many years.

Image courtesy of the Department of Natural Resources.

-FISH-1982-
BLUE-GILLS- 1061
PERCH- 469
PIKE- 77
CRAPPIE- 4
S-BASS- 4
CAT-FISH- 5
TOTAL- 1,620
-FISH-1983-
BLUE-GILLS- 412
PERCH- 720
PIKE- 11
CRAPPIES- 6
S-BASS- 5
CAT-FISH- 193-PERCH-ICE-FISHING 8
4-PIKE-ICE-FISHING
TOTAL-ICE+DOCK- 1,162

-FISH-1974-
BLUE-GILLS- 424
PERCH- 199
PIKE- 8
CRAPPIE- 1
CAT-FISH- 3
N-PIKE- 2
TOTAL-DOCK- 637

Fish count by Zeke Wilson for 1982–1984. Quite a change downward from the previous century.

Image courtesy of Doyne Wilson Hummel.

In 1911 the original hatchery building was renovated, and cement breeding ponds were built. By 1917, production demands had increased enough that this new fish hatchery was built.

Images courtesy of the Department of Natural Resources.

Over the years the state has enacted several rules for fishing such as when anglers could fish, what to keep, and what to fish with. At one point fish "shanties" were banned. (Fish shacks are used in winter for ice fishing.)

Beginning in the late 1800s, the Iowa Fish Commission was formed, followed by the State Game Warden, and then in 1917, the 37th Iowa General Assembly created the State Board of Conservation, later renamed the Iowa Conservation Commission to help conserve natural resources in the state. They properly administer fish and game rules and assess populations and their related habitat. With ever-changing populations and deterioration of habitat, this was a daunting job.

From the 1880s through the 1950s the hatchery raised numerous species including lake trout. In 1963 a new fish hatchery was constructed and efforts were streamlined to raise walleye, musky, tiger musky, and northern pike.
Image courtesy of the Department of Natural Resources.

Of course little boys love it when they catch the "big one" (Brown's Bay, 1956).

Image courtesy of Scott Wendel.

Image courtesy of the Department of Natural Resources.

In 1978, an addition was added to the hatchery to provide more tank space. That hatchery stands unchanged today, but production has dramatically increased, with the facility raising about 100 million walleye, 300,000 northern pike, and 23,000 musky annually.

The science of fish and wildlife management has progressed dramatically since the early days, and most of the regulations in place today to protect and conserve the state's natural resources have been fine-tuned.

Only a few years after common carp were introduced in the late 1880s, it was discovered that these "rough" fish were doing much more harm than good. In 1909, commercial fishing of rough fish was used to try to reduce their numbers, and the catch had good market value. Because the early settlers saw some of the native fish like gar and buffalo as undesirable, these too were classified as rough and removed using gill nets and seining in great numbers.

Images courtesy of the Department of Natural Resources.

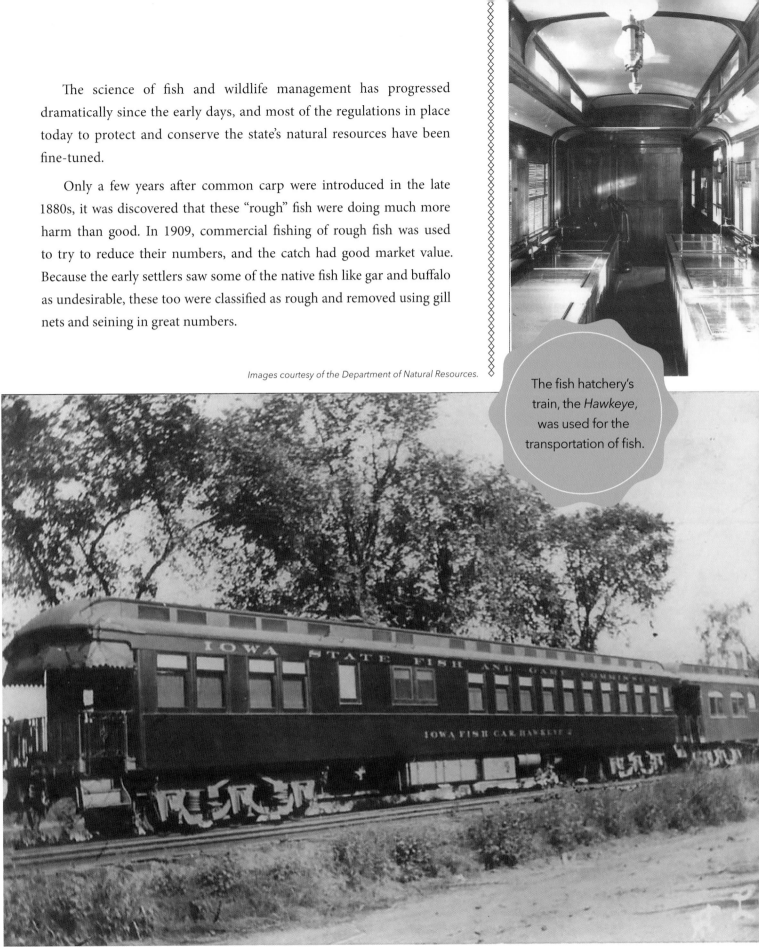

The fish hatchery's train, the *Hawkeye*, was used for the transportation of fish.

This practice was discontinued in 1930 when the commercial program collapsed as the value of fish fell. The Iowa Conservation Commission began its own program in the 1930s with a goal of reducing rough fish numbers, especially common carp, in an attempt to improve game fish numbers. They removed millions of pounds of fish between 1930 and 1972 from the Iowa Great Lakes and had some limited success in improving habitat and game fish numbers.

The State Rough Fish Crew was disbanded in the early 1970s, and a modern commercial program was initiated. This program continues today but the objective shifted from reducing numbers to simply utilizing a renewable resource. Remnants of the old rough fish program can still be seen at Hales Slough on Big Spirit Lake and Garlock Slough on West Okoboji where the old "fish traps" still stand. The old brick Rough Fish Building still stands to the southwest of the Spirit Lake Fish Hatchery. Many of the old tools of the trade are still present in the attic while others can be found in area museums.

Gill nets (as shown) and seines were used during the open water season and also during the winter to cull rough fish. Fish traps were constructed at the entrances of marshes to capture carp moving in to shallow areas to spawn.

To seine in winter, holes would be drilled in the ice about 18 inches apart in a semicircle pattern. The long seine would be threaded along the chain of holes and pulled to a larger open hole where fish were hoisted out of the lake, and then loaded onto a cart or railcar.

Images courtesy of the Department of Natural Resources.

Images courtesy of the Department of Natural Resources.

STATE PARKS

Prior to 1932 all the property around West Lake Okoboji was held in private hands. At that time, a 7.14 acre plot of land was available on the east shore of West Okoboji. This land was originally owned by the Van Steenburg family, D. C. Patterson, and M. L. Kuhn. The state purchased the property for $7,745, and it became Pikes Point State Park.

The State Board of Conservation created Pikes Point State Park in 1932 for the people of Iowa. Besides this shelter, many picnic areas were built. This continues to be a popular family destination.

Image courtesy of Iowa Great Lakes Maritime Museum.

The Iowa Conservation Commission, now the DNR, is responsible for enforcing safety laws on the lakes. The original, and still used, Lake Patrol Station was built by the Milford camp of the CCC on Gull Point in 1935.

Image courtesy of Okoboji Magazine.

KES POINT SHELTER HOUSE W. OKOBOJI LAKE

Many structures built for the state parks in the 1930s were built by the Milford camp of the Civilian Conservation Corps (CCC).

Ft. Des Moines
P.X. Studio
9-4-33

Civilian Conservation Corps
Camp No. 57 - Co. No. 778
Spencer, Ia.

Lt. Theo. Kalakuka
Commanding

Image courtesy of Iowa Great Lakes Maritime Museum.

Clare Wilson State Park is located just to the southeast of the grade between Highway 71 and the former railroad tracks/trail network. The aerial shot shows where what is now the park was at one time water. This space had become a convenient graveyard for old steamships and other unwanted boats and trash. Boats had been towed there and allowed to sink or half sink. Turtles and muskrats made this their home. In 1920 the county maintenance crew burned them to the waterline, but the remnants were still visible. After several years the Okoboji Protective Association requested the area be filled in, and the Conservation Commission then had the retaining wall built.

Along with the patrol station was a large lodge with dining facilities on the shoreline of West Lake Okoboji. These facilities are at the heart of Gull Point State Park. This eighty-two-acre park remains one of the busiest state parks in Iowa. The popular and picturesque lodge, next to the Lake Patrol Station, is reserved every summer weekend for special events.

On West Lake, besides Pikes Point and Gull Point, the state and the CCC created the 2.5-acre Pillsbury Point State Park with a nice walkway and bench.

LAKE PATROL

The very first Lake Patrol boat was acquired in the 1920s. There was a $500 personal donation to buy the materials needed to build the boat. A former worker with the Hafer Boat Works built it. They got the outboard motor through the governor's office. This was a prime example of how the early patrol got things accomplished.

Most needs (radios, boats, for example) were purchased by locals because the Iowa legislature didn't fund them. It became obvious that the patrol needed a way to communicate with the shore. A meeting was set up with a local philanthropist. The need was addressed, discussion was forthcoming, and the donor provided a much better radio operation than had been asked for. All because it was good for the lake.

The Lake Patrol previously operated with a five-man team. Most patrol officers were teachers or college students on break for the summer. In 2005, Michael Brosnahan was killed by a drunken boater. This brought a lot of attention to the safety of the lakes and caused the DNR to add officers as well as create a night speed limit. Today there are two full-time officers with an additional eight to ten college students patrolling the lakes in the summer.

Former Lake Patrol officer Bill Maas shared some amazing stories about the patrol. Maas had always heard that if you shout out about halfway between Manhattan Beach and Echo Bay, your voice would echo back. He took a patrol boat out one night and tried to get his voice to echo. Well, he was radioed to come to the aid of a boater in the Echo Bay area. Seems that residents heard his echoing voice and thought a boater was stranded.

Image courtesy of Okoboji Tourism and Blue Water Ventures, David Thoreson.

He also addressed the rumor about quicksand at Pikes Point. Kids were told to avoid Pikes Point because there was quicksand in the area. Not so, but a strong wind can create very strong undertow that has caused several drownings, so beware!

Lake Patrol watching as the Arnolds Park/ Okoboji Fire and Rescue are practicing with their water nozzle.

IOWA GREAT LAKES SANITARY DISTRICT

Where you have people, you have waste in the form of trash and, well, human waste. Wastewater was actually discussed as long ago as 1906. This was at the first Okoboji Protective Association meeting. In 1915 residents and visitors complained about the noxious smell of algae blooms, thought to be caused by sewage. At that time, Lakeside Labs urged residents to install "proper earth toilets" or outhouses. The thing was, many still drained into the lakes. In 1927 the Department of Health did a fairly comprehensive study, but nothing was done until 1937, when the largest sanitary sewer project in Iowa was begun.

The Sanitary Sewer System consisted of a sewer line from south of Big Spirit Lake, through Spirit Lake, Okoboji, Arnolds Park, and into the treatment plant north of Milford. Treated water would be discharged into Milford Creek.

Sewer collection finally looped around West Lake in the early 1960s. Big Spirit Lake had lines started in the 1940s and was finally completed in the 1970s. The last lines installed went around East Okoboji from 1978 to 1980. (This is why East Lake was so very green, and water-skiers had to take a shower afterward.) Since these lines were completed, the water quality has markedly improved.

One of the planning maps used for the sewer system. The project was extended to include the east side of West Lake Okoboji, and the plant was brought online November 8, 1939.

Installation work for the many, many miles of sewer pipes and lift stations needed for the region.

Images courtesy of the Iowa Great Lakes Sanitary District.

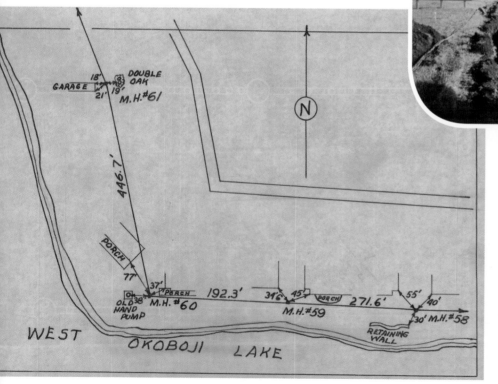

Image courtesy of the Iowa Great Lakes Sanitary District.

LAKESIDE LAB

The Lakeside Laboratory shall afford to all interested, for once at least a chance to see the real world, nature alive, accomplishing her miracles in their own silent splendor, often needing not, for the student's appreciation, the voice of interpreter or teacher…—Thomas Huston Macbride, Founder, Iowa Lakeside Laboratory

One of the greatest assets of the lake, and Iowa, is Lakeside Laboratory. But first some history.

Nearly two decades had passed since Dr. Thomas Huston Macbride, professor and later president of the University of Iowa, first visited and fell under the charm and beauty of the Okoboji region in the late 1800s. Back then, northwest Iowa, compared to the eastern part of the state, still remained somewhat of a frontier. Often accompanied by his colleagues Samuel Calvin and Bohumil Shimek, Macbride was one of the first scientists to explore and describe the region both as university research and under contract with the Iowa Geologic Survey.

Image courtesy of Lakeside Lab.

Dr. Thomas Huston Macbride in 1909, the year Iowa Lakeside Laboratory was established.

Upon legislative mandate, the Iowa Geologic Survey had contracted with Professor Macbride, and other leading Iowa scientists, to investigate and inventory the soils, flora, and fauna of the region for their practical importance and scientific interest.

Images courtesy of University of Iowa Library Archives.

Professor Macbride's expertise was vast. He taught botany, zoology, and geology at the University of Iowa (then called State University of Iowa) where he became professor in 1871, and its eleventh president in 1914. He authored numerous scientific papers on topics ranging from slime molds, fungi, and general botany to geology and paleobotany. He held a BA in mathematics and languages and was proficient in five languages.

Lauded by his colleague Bohumil Shimek as "Iowa's Dean of Conservation," Macbride was also an avid conservationist. He was the architect of Iowa's county conservation board system, instrumental in the formation of Iowa's state parks, and a founding member of the Iowa Academy of Science.

Yet perhaps Professor Macbride's greatest legacy is as a visionary educator and leader. A masterful teacher, he understood back then what modern brain research is telling us today: that authentic and deep learning happens best with hands-on experiences. He lamented that the teaching of natural sciences in schools and universities was "too formal, too artificial" and too much based upon pickled specimens or preserved material.

Inspired by the region's diverse landforms and aquatic and terrestrial habitats, Professor Macbride and his colleagues hatched a dream to create a biological field station there for "the study of nature *in* nature."

Image courtesy of David Boot album, State Historical Society of Iowa, Iowa City.

Image courtesy of University of Iowa Library Archives.

Shimek Lab.

Image courtesy of Lakeside Lab.

Macbride Lab.

Students in the field at Lakeside Laboratory. "Field conditions could not be brought to the classroom," Macbride determined that "the laboratory must be brought to the field."

Images courtesy of University of Iowa Library Archives.

◇◇

Female students stayed in tents or in nearby farmhouses in the early years of Lakeside Lab's operations. The rental for a tent was 75 cents per occupant.

Image courtesy of Lakeside Lab.

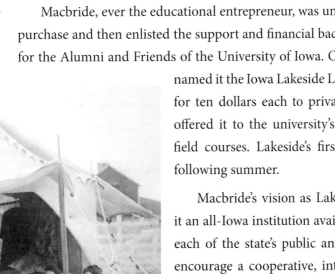

Thus, in 1908 when a five-acre tract of land on Little Miller's Bay, the former E. B. Smith property, came up for sale, Macbride jumped at the chance to purchase it. However, a statutory provision in the Iowa constitution disallowed the establishment of a university "branch" in any other form or location than Iowa City.

Macbride, ever the educational entrepreneur, was undaunted. He secured an option to purchase and then enlisted the support and financial backing of "Old Gold," the nickname for the Alumni and Friends of the University of Iowa. Old Gold formed a stock company, named it the Iowa Lakeside Laboratory Association, sold shares for ten dollars each to privately purchase the land, and then offered it to the university's science department for summer field courses. Lakeside's first academic season was held the following summer.

Macbride's vision as Lakeside's first director was to make it an all-Iowa institution available to students and faculty from each of the state's public and private universities in order to encourage a cooperative, intercollegial learning environment. In its first year, fourteen institutions were represented at Lakeside. Today, this spirit of open collegiality remains one of Lakeside's chief attributes as it continues to draw students, researchers, and faculty not only from across Iowa but from across the country and around the world.

From its very inception, students and faculty alike have described Lakeside's learning environment as exceptional and often life changing. Classes are small, allowing freer dialogue among professors and students. During meal times and late into the night, often around a camp fire, students compare and contrast their knowledge, and at the same time form deep friendships that often become life-long.

Learning is holistic and field-oriented: no matter the topic of study, students gain a deep understanding of the interconnectivity of physical and biological worlds, the impact of geology on soils, topography and hydrological features, and in turn their impact on plant and animal life, harkening back to the early days of Macbride and his colleagues when the physical and natural sciences were practiced more under the single discipline of natural history than the separate disciplines they are considered today.

Additionally, students get a real-world understanding of the practice of science, that is much more than memorizing terms and concepts, it is being in the field: observing, asking questions, collecting data, analysis, discussion, revision—and not always in that order. Then there is the environment of Lakeside itself: its lakeshore setting with its classrooms not under a single roof but in small labs scattered across the campus, each devoted to a particular topic of study, and encouraging the sense of immersion in nature as one walks across campus from living area to classroom surrounded by trees or prairie or a sparkling view of West Lake Okoboji.

After its founding in 1909, the Iowa Lakeside Laboratory Association continued to operate Lakeside until 1936 when the Association deeded the property to the state of Iowa Executive Council. From 1936 to 1947, Lakeside was run by a board of managers represented by the State Conservation Commission (today the Iowa Department of Natural Resources), the State Board of Education (now the Iowa Board of Regents), the Iowa Lakeside Association, the U.S. Fish and Wildlife Service, and the University of Iowa.

Through donations spearheaded by the Friends of Lakeside Lab, the completion of the Waitt Lab in 1998, on schedule and under budget, ushered in a new era for Lakeside. Equipped with the Bovbjerg Water Chemistry Lab, a science-teaching lab, community classroom, and offices, Lakeside now had the infrastructure to implement the Friends' vision for pre-K through 12 programming, outreach programs and water quality monitoring and research.

Image courtesy of Lakeside Lab.

In 1947 the board of managers structure was dissolved and the Iowa State Board of Education took responsibility for Lakeside. Since then, Lakeside has been part of the Iowa Board of Regents system and operated jointly by Iowa's three state universities—with the University of Iowa acting as the administrative home for the lab in most years.

In the interim, Lakeside property increased from its original five acres to include additional purchases made in 1928 and 1978. The present campus, managed as a nature reserve, includes 140 acres of lakeshore, savanna, and prairie habitat.

Lakeside has survived several administrative challenges since its inception: wartimes, the Great Depression, and the original Iowa statue barring the establishment of Lakeside as a university branch. Yet with each challenge, Macbride's dream has been born anew, drawing forth a new generation of students, researchers, and supporters. The formation of the Friends of Lakeside Lab in the 1990s is the most recent example.

In 2008 Lakeside entered into partnership with the State Hygienic Lab, Iowa's public health and environmental laboratory, to operate the Bovbjerg Water Chemistry Lab as an Environmental Protection Agency-certified facility. The same year Lakeside became a Regents Resource Center, broadening its natural science offerings to include artist and writer residencies and the Okoboji Entrepreneurship Institute.

Today, if Thomas Huston Macbride were to come back to life and stroll about the Lakeside campus, he would be amazed at what his vision to create a place for "the study of nature in nature" has wrought.

Image courtesy of Lakeside Lab.

School-year programs, teacher trainings, science camps, family programs, and volunteer opportunities as well as public lectures and forums on environmental topics supplement traditional academic and research programs.

Image courtesy of Lakeside Lab.

Always a firm believer that science should be accessible to people of all ages and backgrounds, Professor Macbride would be delighted to observe not only college students but also four- and five-year-olds conducting investigations in the prairie grasses and along the lakeshore during Frog Camp.

Images courtesy of Lakeside Lab.

Macbride would certainly join with families as an eager participant in Lakeside's weekly Wild Wednesday family science programs. He would learn about citizen science—something unheard of in his time—after running into community volunteers from the Cooperative Lakes Area Monitoring Project as they returned to the Lakeside from collecting lake water samples, and sit down for coffee, rolls and philosophical discussions with the Coffee and Grounds volunteers after a morning's work pulling invasive species or collecting native seed. A visionary educator who understood the importance of hands-on learning, Macbride would be impressed by Lakeside's pre-K through 12 learning immersion programs, and to learn that educators from across northwest Iowa attend Lakeside for professional development in best science practices.

Thanks to the tenacity of Macbride's vision and the support of the Friends of Lakeside Lab, Lakeside has survived for over a century. Yet, as Michael J. Lannoo, longtime faculty member and alum observed, today's humanity needs places like Lakeside to survive. With the growing concern about children's disconnect with nature and its impact on their socioemotional, cognitive, and physical development, places like Lakeside can introduce and instill in learners from a very young age a positive, life-long relationship with nature.

And with today's huge array of environmental challenges—pollution, toxic waste, habitat loss, invasive species, climate change, and health impacts of chemicals released into environment—field stations are needed to study these impacts in nature, especially places such as Lakeside with long histories of data collection. "In the Midwest," writes Lannoo, "this place is the Iowa Lakeside Lab, situated in the remarkable community called Okoboji."

EXIT

Image courtesy of Lakeside Lab and Greg Drees.

[In writing about Lakeside Lab, Jane Shuttleworth provided this information with expertise and enthusiasm. Faculty member Mike Lannoo and his interns, Dakota Keller and Bruce McWilliams, were also helpful in providing information and photographs.]

DREDGING/CANAL PROJECTS

Can humankind create more lakeshore property? Should it? Three significant dredging/canal digging projects have taken place on West Lake Okoboji.

The first project was supposed to create an "American Venice." In 1911, J. A. Beck, founder of The Inn, and H. E. Mills of Spirit Lake, wanted to develop 1,000 acres of lakefront property between Miller's Bay and Emerson Bay.

The dream was to create 500 lakefront lots sitting along a series of canals. The lots sold poorly and eventually became overgrown. The state kept them cleared for several years but that became onerous. Private individuals took over the job, but it became too much for them as well. Today the area is quite wild, and it is best to take only a kayak, and plenty of mosquito repellant, through much of the system.

In May 1928, Mr. and Mrs. Alex Percival contracted with the *Sioux City Tribune* to develop and promote their 178 acres of farmland at the north end of West Okoboji. They named the development Triboji.

By 1930 fifty summer cottages had been built, and a year later over 530 lots sold. (Considering this was during the Depression, this was quite an accomplishment!) The original agreement was that the *Sioux City Tribune* (now *Sioux City Journal*) would help develop and promote the project, and promote they did.

Teresa Garvey, granddaughter of Alex Percival, said a big picnic, rodeo, and a beauty contest had all been held to promote the property. The contract with the *Tribune* has long since expired. Most of the property is now owned by private individuals. Hedge Row cottages sit on some of the land, and there are also some parks. The little island created by the dredging of Lazy Lagoon is still owned by the Percival family.

The last dredging project to create additional waterfront lots was announced by developers Nodland and Scheppmann in September 1970. In January of the following year, the plat for "Okoboji Harbour" at the north end of the lake had been filed and approved. By that fall homes were being built. This has been a successful development.

So, can this be replicated? Probably not. DNR Iowa law allows for existing canals to be maintained. No new canals can be excavated unless the canal is constructed by the state, a county, or a municipality on public ground. The purpose of the activity must be for public access not private access. Of course, this assumes a favorable environmental review. If the proposed construction were determined to be detrimental, it would not be allowed. All of the review standards in Iowa code would need to be met.

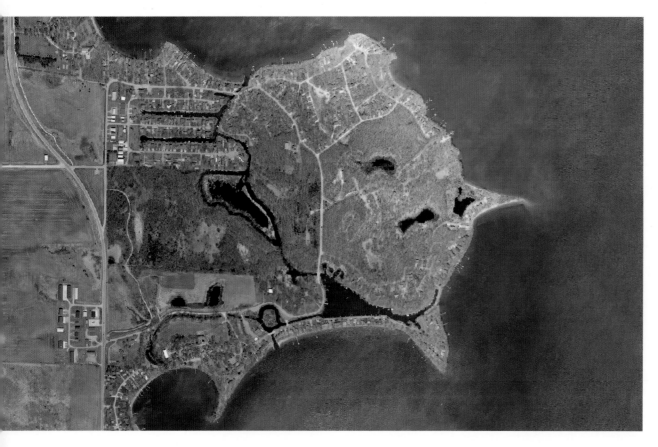

This project connecting Miller's Bay with Emerson Bay was called Lakewood Park. Five openings into the lake were dug to connect the canals. The canals varied in width from eight to twelve feet and were three miles long.

Image courtesy of the Department of Natural Resources.

CANAL SCENE

VESTERGAARDS LAKE SHORE RE
MILFORD, IOWA D-281

View from the Lakewood Park canals.

Dredging the canal to keep it open.

TAKE YOUR FAMILY AND DRIVE TO--

TRIBOJI BEACH

THE SIOUX CITY TRIBUNE'S SUMMER RESORT ON THE NORTH SHORE OF WEST OKOBOJI LAKE

This Beautiful resort is located on State Highway Number 9, four miles west of Spirit Lake, Iowa. It is bounded on three sides by graveled roads and every lot is on a graveled street. Do not fear the rain—the roads are always good. Those familiar with the price and location of lake lots wonder why The Tribune can sell choice lots for only $94. The Tribune is not selling Triboji lots for monetary gain, but as a goodwill builder. Triboji Beach is a monument to the benevolence and prestige of our great newspaper. Triboji lots are being sold at what they will cost The Tribune when all improvements, purchase price of the land, advertising and sales expense have been paid.

INVEST **$94**.00   PLUS A $5 Subscription to The Sioux City Tribune   In a Triboji Beach Lot

You'll never regret it. You'll never miss the money. You'll not only make money on the investment, but you'll have a place to take the family over week-ends. You can pitch a tent on your own ground or build an economical cottage.

GOOD FISHING, GOOD HUNTING, GOOD BATHING, GOOD BOATING, GOLFING

A Real Time All the Time

$30 DOWN, $10 PER MONTH

TERMS-- Without Interest

Beach Dedicated to Public
Over a mile of fine white sand beach, 100 feet back from the water, is dedicated to Triboji Beach lot owners, thus assuring the same privileges to all residents, no matter where their lot may be located. This will be a permanent park open for Triboji Beach residents.

Good Railroad Service
The main line of the Chicago, Rock Island and Pacific Railroad, from Sioux Falls, S.

D., to Chicago, passes within six blocks of Triboji Beach. Regular stops are made at this point.

Golf and Steamer Service
A public golf course is only seven blocks away on State Highway No. 9. Lake steamers make regular trips to the beach, where is located the largest dock on the lake. Triboji Beach is always cooled with gentle breezes that sweep across the lake.

REPRESENTATIVES AT TRIBOJI BEACH WILL GIVE YOU A REAL WELCOME. WE WANT YOU AND YOUR FAMILY TO HAVE A GOOD TIME. VISIT OUR BEACH ANY TIME.

For Further Information Call at

The Sioux City Tribune

SIOUX CITY, IOWA

A twenty-five-foot lot cost $94. This was promoted as a place for a common person to own a piece of paradise.

As part of the Triboji development, the Lazy Lagoon was dredged, providing additional space for boats as well as a small island off West Lake Okoboji.

WIND TURBINES

The first wind turbine in the area was built at the Spirit Lake High School. A few years later they added a second turbine. According to an article in 2005, the school was saving $26,000 annually with their two wind turbines. Electric companies now utilize the wind power to the benefit of the state and their people.

Throughout history one thing seems to run true. The health of the lakes is the most crucial aspect of this area. It is why the Native Americans found this place special and why people flock to the area now. Ecology is more than just how the natural system works, it also encompasses how we interact with our lakes. Promoting a healthy ecology means working toward protecting the land and the water and all the life living in it. The lakes community has always stepped up to that challenge as they work to pass on this treasure to the next generation of lake lovers.

Today, multiple wind turbines can be seen looking west over the lake.

Image courtesy of Okoboji Tourism and Blue Water Ventures, David Thoreson.

Did you know?

Diver's Den and the Okoboji Protective Association sponsored an environmental clean-up day for divers in 1970. About fifty divers participated and brought up loads of automobile tires, bottles, cans, even a 16-foot rowboat and a diamond ring.

LAKE BOTTOM CLEANUP — Some of the junk cleaned off the bottom of West Okoboji Lake Friday is displayed at Diver's Den in Okoboji for Congressman Wiley Mayne of Sioux City, second from left, holding an old truck transmission. Scuba divers spent the day in the "environmental clean up" sponsored by the Okoboji Protective Association. From left are Jay Hoselton, Mayne, Rich Rierson and Bob Eaves.

Image courtesy of Rob Eves.

STORMS AND TRAGEDIES

Okoboji is an idyllic place, but not always. The lake story would not be complete without including storms and tragedies. When storm clouds roll in or tragic events take place, the community comes together and gets through it. That IS part of what Okoboji is so much about.

Storm clouds gather.

Image courtesy of Explore Okoboji.

STORMS

Storms can be wonderful to watch on the porch of a cottage, but they can turn frightening fast. The power of wind and rain have dealt Okoboji several blows over the years.

On the afternoon of April 30, 1936, a strong tornado struck Terrace Park. The storm traveled for miles. A school bus loaded with children miraculously made it without any injuries. The driver, Zeke Wilson, drove the bus into a ravine and told the children to hunker down. They were saved, but almost everything else around them was destroyed.

On Wednesday, July 4, 1962, the lakes received 10.5 inches of rain. The lake rose 18 inches and inundated the docks, hoists, boats, and especially low-land property. To add insult to injury, the area had hurricane force winds the following Saturday, July 7. Waves on the lake were seven feet tall with winds 70 miles per hour.

Someone had a sense of humor after the tornado of April 30, 1936.

Image courtesy of Don McCulloch.

The Casino at Terrace Park, very sturdily built, made it, but all the beautiful landscaping that Terrace Park was known for was uprooted by the 1936 tornado.

Image courtesy of the Iowa Great Lakes Maritime Museum.

The erosion was unimaginable following the storms of 1962. The bank on Echo Bay collapsed. Trees and other debris were out in the lake. Damage was in the millions. These photographs show before, and after damage, to the Morgan property.

Images courtesy of Bowers/Mendenhall family and Dickinson County News.

Then the Okoboji tornado of the century hit on June 13, 1968.

The author remembers the 1968 tornado: It was a strange afternoon. Eldon Kanago, the weatherman-extraordinaire at KICD AM radio station in Spencer, was broadcasting about the tornados that were hitting nearby Pipestone, Minnesota. I was sitting on the lakeshore bank with my mom and sister watching funnels drop out of the clouds. My mother told me it would hail before a tornado would hit.

Suddenly it started to hail and the sirens went off. Our cottage was one of the few with a basement, so many neighbors with their pets came down. The storm hit. I went outside with my dad after the funnel passed. Mom went upstairs to refill the ice bucket. (With all the neighbors we turned it into a party.) She heard a train, but they had stopped traveling through Okoboji years ago. I happened to look down at Given's Point. There was a tremendous funnel of water that seemed 100 feet tall. (Bruce Smith, who was down on Smith's Bay, said he could see the lake bottom when the water funnel moved toward Arnolds Park.)

We rushed back to our basement. That was the funnel that flattened Fillenwarth Beach Resort, the amusement park, downtown Arnolds Park, Boys Town, Vern & Coila's restaurant, and much more. What was incredible is that no lives were lost. Credit is clearly due to the constant broadcasting from KICD and the national weather bureau.

The Ferris wheel was toppled.

TORNADO

JUNE 1968

Special Supplement to
Spirit Lake Beacon
Milford Mail
Lake Park News

Your Dickinson County Newspapers

Cover of the special TORNADO issue.

The *Queen*, which was the fireboat at the time, was severely damaged.

The property on Terrace Park, now owned by Boys Town, was once again hit.

Images courtesy of Dickinson County News.

Much of Fillenwarth Beach Resort was leveled.

After several mild-mannered weather years, the storm of June 28, 1993, hit.

To set the stage, the lake was already quite high due to an unseasonably wet spring. Two storms moved through, dumping about four inches of rain each. The water came down so hard the roads were turned into streams. The lake level went up 24 inches, which was then 51 inches above normal. Docks were just about level with the lake water. Dock owners put large trash cans on them and filled them with water to try to keep the docks from floating away. (If they already hadn't.)

Significant erosion was a concern, especially with sightseers paying no attention to the wave action they were creating as they motor-boated around. At first the DNR did nothing. They had no legal action they could take. After a while the patrol initiated a "No Wake" zone within 300 feet of the shores. This was expanded as needed. Many property owners had their boats and docks completely removed. Others had everything raised. New road curbs, and the storm sewer system, were the result of this flooding. It was a rather quiet summer after the storm with so few boats on the lake.

More recently, straight-line winds have created problems.

Flooding at Fisherman's Wharf in 1993.

The Ritz and Funtime Rentals flooding.

Images courtesy of Fred Cerwick.

Boats caught up under canopies couldn't get out.

Water level at the bridge.

The flood impacted the amusement park. Sandbagging tried to protect the Legend roller coaster.

Image courtesy of Iowa Great Lakes Maritime Museum.

Flooding of a private home.

Image courtesy of Fred Cerwick.

Image courtesy of Russ Oechslin, Sioux City Journal.

Just a few years after devastating winds in 2010, the area received up to 70 mph winds on Monday, June 16, 2014.

Image courtesy of Explore Okoboji.

Late-night storm warnings were issued by the National Weather Service on Saturday July 17, 2010. The winds began to pick up around 10:30 p.m. Within the next forty-five minutes, the lake witnessed over 70 mph winds that blew everything south toward Terrace Park. (Some said the winds were 100 mph.) Boats, and anything that could blow, were tossed on the southern shore or swept away.

TRAGEDIES

The most infamous tragedy was the collision of two speed boats, *The Zipper* and *Miss Thriller*, which occurred after dark about 9:30 p.m. on Sunday, July 28, 1929.

Miss Thriller, a super-fast sea-sled-type boat with speeds up to 50 mph (even though the lake speed limit was 45 mph and cars in those days could barely go 30 mph). During WWI she served as a submarine chaser off New York Harbor. Later she was used to chase rum runners on the St. Lawrence River during Prohibition. She would take visitors out for a thrill ride. That fateful night *The Zipper*, a slower-speed excursion boat, hit *Miss Thriller* and tore a large hole in her aft.

Miss Thriller had fifteen on board and nine lost their lives. All nine passengers on *The Zipper* made it ashore. The case was taken to court, appealed, had a change of venue, and in the end no one was convicted.

Nine on board *Miss Thriller* died in a 1929 boat crash.

Image courtesy of Iowa Great Lake Maritime Museum.

A beached *Miss Thriller* after the tragic crash.

Image courtesy of Iowa Great Lakes Maritime Museum.

Divers searching for *Miss Thriller*.

Image courtesy of O'Farrell family.

One of the saddest lake drownings occurred on Saturday, July 14, 1934. A group of young women from Orange City, Iowa, were walking along the submerged, mossy rocks at Pillsbury Point. They were all holding hands when one slipped. One-by-one the girls followed the first into the water. The last two in line were saved, but five others, including their chaperone, didn't make it.

What came to be called "The Brosnahan Incident" occurred in 2005. Dr. and Mrs. Brosnahan were out in a friend's boat late at night when an intoxicated young man was speeding in another boat and hit their craft. Dr. Brosnahan was killed and his wife badly injured.

Because of this high-speed accident, the DNR petitioned that, "No vessels, except authorized emergency vessels, shall be operated at speeds greater than 25 miles per hour at any time between the hours of one half hour after sunset and sunrise on all lakes located in Dickinson County." This incident also resulted in additional patrol officers on the lake.

SEASONS

Okoboji geographically celebrates all four distinctive seasons, each with its natural wonders surrounding the lake and lake activities and surprisingly picturesque settings to capture family memories.

Image courtesy of Fred Cerwick.

SPRING

Spring is synonymous with mud. It always seems to be late in arriving at the lakes. It is a time of finding out just which plants survived the winter, pulling up volunteer oak trees due to those pesky acorns, and getting in touch with friends and neighbors to find out just when they will be back for the season. But for the dock, hoist, and boat companies, the rush is on to get the structures back into the lake.

First they have to wait until the ice is out. Then the barges are prepared and gassed up. It can't be windy where the docks are being installed, so you can tell where they will be working by the wind direction. The workers always pray for an early spring so they have more time to get everyone's dock in. On those late "ice out" years, it is quite common to find short dock starts installed just so the owners can get their hoists and boats in. The rest of the length and shape of the dock will be installed as soon as the builders can get to them.

Early in May, the lake hosts Walleye Weekend, which is signaled by the early-morning sounds of fishing boats. Close to Memorial Day, retail shops begin to open, as do the seasonal restaurants.

When the *Queen II* begins her runs, and the Ferris wheel begins to turn at Arnolds Park, summer is just around the corner.

Now the dock is in, but the dock builders need to contact the boat hoist installer. They try to follow each other as quickly as possible. As soon as the hoist is in, the boats can be hauled out of storage and put in the water.

Image courtesy of Kooima Lakes Service, Inc.

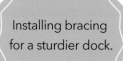

Installing bracing for a sturdier dock.

Image courtesy of Okoboji Tourism and Blue Water Ventures, David Thoreson.

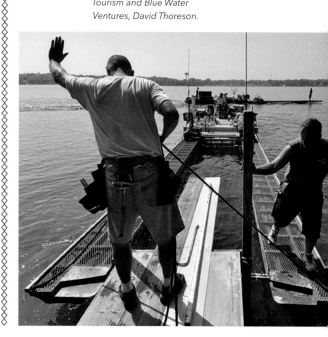

Consider that every dock on the lake must be put in. Most owners want them installed *right away*. It takes 2.5 hours with a crew of four to install a typical wooden dock. The posts are 4 x 4's and the planks are 1 x 12's. Many docks are built with custom built "U" shaped barges, like this one by Kenny Halibur.

Image courtesy of Okoboji Tourism and Blue Water Ventures, David Thoreson.

SUMMER

Warmth and the "summer people" arrive—whether for the season, a week, or a weekend. Stores and restaurants have all opened. The sun stays up until after 9:00 p.m. in July. Wind is frequent, and storms are not unusual. Water activities abound, whether vacationers are on the water or in the water.

There is nothing more amazing than watching a night lightning storm roll in over the lake.

Image courtesy of Neal Christensen.

Neighbors on Des Moines Beach put together a raft held up by an oil barrel at all corners, then added a "diving platform" (1913).

Image courtesy of Martha Green.

The most popular water activity has always been swimming, but can you imagine wearing this? "Ladies' apparel for a 'dip' included long black stockings, a full skirt extending below the knees, bathing shoes, and a large sun hat," as quoted from an article in the *Des Moines Register*. As late as 1921 a woman would be fined $2 to $100 or 30 days in jail if she was over the age of fifteen and appeared on the street without an over-garment fully covering the body from shoulder to knee (image from 1885).

Image courtesy of Martha Green.

Toboggan water slides were the first "constructed" activities on the lakes. These were massive and involved putting a large sled on the track and sliding down (Arnold's Park, 1910).
Image courtesy of Luckybreak/Okoboji.

Bob Mandelbaum gave swimming classes for years from his home on Des Moines Beach. These were his 1954 students.
Image courtesy of Iowa Great Lakes Maritime Museum.

Image courtesy of Lesleigh Buck.

Ready, Set, GO! There were always races from dock to dock at the lake.
Image courtesy of Lesleigh Buck.

Fun in the water. Rafts were great, but look out a bit farther. The black inner-tubes were tradition. Old car tires had these inside of them. They were then repurposed for swimming use. You could always tell a swimmer who had used an inner-tube because the black would rub off on the body.

For 25 cents you could rent a water bike at the Bilyeu Water Bikes in front of Bennit's Park (1957).

Image courtesy of Iowa Great Lakes Maritime Museum.

Green's rowboat was rigged with a sail (1912).

Image courtesy of Martha Green.

A century ago, "Most of these launches were 20 feet to 24 feet in length, strip-constructed of cedar or cypress lumber, round bottom with stern built to a point or dove-tailed and when in operation left no wake or disturbance in the water," according to Fred Wilson. A reversible propeller was used in the old models. Later, the engine was moved forward with decking built over the engines.

In about 1920 launches were made with a V-bottom design. This allowed them to ride the surface of the water instead of pushing through it. Then came inboard/outboard motors and boats made of fiberglass.

What people do with their boats has also changed, yet a leisure sail or a thrilling speed-boat ride is still enjoyed.

Lake Okoboji, Iowa.

Sailboats and rowboats were common on the lake (1907).

Image courtesy of Luckybreak/Okoboji.

"Most boats, *called launches at that time,* were built by John Hafer of Spirit Lake. Several were built here at Wilsons by my Uncle Oliver. Arp Bros. built several and a few were shipped in," according to Fred Wilson in *The Girl on a Horse*. Pictured is the *Merry Macs*, a Hafer launch in front of the Okoboji Yacht Club off Pikes Point.

Image courtesy of Iowa Great Lakes Maritime Museum.

A narrow launch in 1910.

Image courtesy of Martha Green.

SLALOM SKIER JAY HOSELTON TUNES UP FOR AUGUST 23 TOURNEY

Second Slalom Tourney Aug. 23

Water skiing has long been a favorite with Iowa Great Lakes residents and visitors, and slalom skiing - competitive skiing with one ski - is rapidly increasing in popularity among both young and old alike.

In July, co-sponsors Diver's Den, Incorporated, and The Cove held the first Iowa Great Lakes Slalom Tournament at The Narrows on East Okoboji Lake. Trophies and medals were awarded to winners.

Greeted with ample success in the initial endeavor, The Cove and Diver's Den are sponsoring a second Iowa Great Lakes Slalom Tournament Sunday, August 23. Junior boys and boys events will be held at 10 a.m. with the men's division scheduled for 1 p.m.

Site for the tournament will again be The Narrows. Those interested may register at either The Cove or Diver's Den, with Scott Post or Jay Hoselton, co-directors of the event. The tournament is open to the public, admission free.

Image courtesy of Rob Eves.

In 1971 the first "Great Okoboji 2 x 4' Regatta" was held. The rafts had to be built with only 2 x 4' lumber, a maximum of two sheets of plywood and Styrofoam. They were powered by oars, paddles or sails, but all had to be homemade.

Image courtesy of Rob Eves and Dickinson County News.

If you were a good skier, you slalomed. There were even tournaments held, like this one from 1971.

On the Fourth of July, local musician Damon Dotson puts on a free afternoon concert in Miller's Bay. The floating crowds are enormous.

Image courtesy of Bob Trader.

Water skiing or slaloming has mostly been replaced with wake boarding.

Image courtesy of Mau Marine.

"Maui Mats" are the rage. They are like a floatable dock extension or an extra-large foam raft, often found stowed on the back of a boat when not in use.

Image courtesy of Mau Marine.

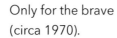

Only for the brave (circa 1970).

Image courtesy of Rob Eves.

In 2015 people surfed behind boats built to create a large wake.

Image courtesy of Okoboji Tourism and Blue Water Ventures, David Thoreson.

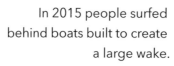

Image courtesy of Mau Marine.

Boaters decorate their boats to participate in the festivities on the Fourth of July.

Tom Kuhlman designed and built the barge that holds the ever-popular fireworks display on the Fourth of July and other evenings. The lake is filled with hundreds of boats. Most have their radios tuned to KUOO to listen to the simulcast music. The Pledge of Allegiance and National Anthem are played just before the display.

Image courtesy of Okoboji Tourism and Blue Water Ventures, David Thoreson.

The Point to Point Swim and the University of Okoboji triathlon illustrate just a few of the organized events throughout the summer.

Images courtesy of Okoboji Tourism and Blue Water Ventures, David Thoreson.

Image courtesy of Okoboji Tourism and Blue Water Ventures, David Thoreson.

Smith's Bay on a busy summer weekend. Congestion is common with the traffic to and from East Okoboji.

Families with young children (or kids of any age) love to be pulled behind boats in special tubes. Jet skis, paddleboards, and kayaks are also popular alternative modes of water transportation. Adventurous souls pay to have a boat pull them up into the sky over the lake, called parasailing.

But not everything is water dependent.

Image courtesy of Okoboji Tourism and Blue Water Ventures, David Thoreson.

The number of fun things occurring on the Green Space at the park is limited only to the number of days in the summer. These include, but are not limited to, concerts, Art in the Park, Motor Cycle Show/Victory Rally, and Vettes in the Park.

Concerts are held every summer weekend on Preservation Plaza at Arnolds Amusement Park.

Image courtesy of Okoboji Tourism.

Image courtesy of Okoboji Tourism and Blue Water Ventures, David Thoreson.

Bicycling is especially popular and there are a number of improved trails to walk, bike, or roller skate/roller blade upon. The University of Okoboji Campus Ride, always on the last Saturday in June, is a favorite with their 25-, 50-, and 100-mile routes.

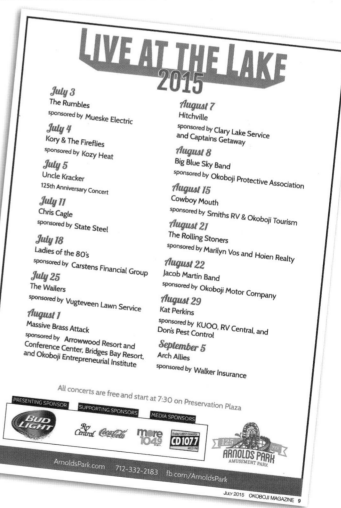

LIVE AT THE LAKE 2015

July 3
The Rumbles
sponsored by Mueske Electric

July 4
Kory & The Fireflies
sponsored by Kozy Heat

July 5
Uncle Kracker
125th Anniversary Concert

July 11
Chris Cagle
sponsored by State Steel

July 18
Ladies of the 80's
sponsored by Carstens Financial Group

July 25
The Wailers
sponsored by Vugteveen Lawn Service

August 1
Massive Brass Attack
sponsored by Arrowwood Resort and Conference Center, Bridges Bay Resort, and Okoboji Entrepreneurial Institute

August 7
Hitchville
sponsored by Clary Lake Service and Captains Getaway

August 8
Big Blue Sky Band
sponsored by Okoboji Protective Association

August 15
Cowboy Mouth
sponsored by Smiths RV & Okoboji Tourism

August 21
The Rolling Stoners
sponsored by Marilyn Vos and Hoien Realty

August 22
Jacob Martin Band
sponsored by Okoboji Motor Company

August 29
Kat Perkins
sponsored by KUOO, RV Central, and Don's Pest Control

September 5
Arch Allies
sponsored by Walker Insurance

All concerts are free and start at 7:30 on Preservation Plaza

PRESENTING SPONSOR   SUPPORTING SPONSORS   MEDIA SPONSORS

BUD LIGHT   Rp Central   Coca Cola   more 104.9   CD 107.7   ARNOLDS PARK AMUSEMENT PARK

ArnoldsPark.com   712-332-2183   fb.com/ArnoldsPark

JULY 2015 OKOBOJI MAGAZINE **9**

The University of Okoboji hosts homecoming every year on the third weekend in July, and the following weekend, Mau Marine hosts the Iowa Great Lakes Antique & Classic Wooden Boat Show.

Image courtesy of Okoboji Tourism and Blue Water Ventures, David Thoreson.

Runs, marathons, and a triathlon attract avid runners during the summer.

Image courtesy of Okoboji Tourism and Blue Water Ventures, David Thoreson.

There is even a tractor parade!

Image courtesy of Okoboji Tourism and Blue Water Ventures, David Thoreson.

Did you know?

The 2003 homecoming fireworks show on West Lake Okoboji had a misfired rocket that fell back on the barge and caused the remaining fireworks to explode. No one was hurt, but Tom Kuhlman retired from shooting off the fireworks after that show. (However he did build the new fireworks barge.)

Images courtesy of Fred Cerwick.

AUTUMN

Summer may be winding down, but autumn is a favorite time of the year at the lake. Most of the summer residents have gone home. The days are typically dry and warm and the nights just right for a fire pit and windows left ajar. You can still smell leaves burning on calm days.

Neighbors take more walks or rake up the massive amounts of acorns that have fallen. It is a bittersweet time as we say temporary goodbyes to the lake until next time.

Image courtesy of Kooima Lakes Service, Inc.

This is again a busy time of activity for those responsible for docks and boats. All hoists and docks, except those in a few areas, must be removed. If they are not, there is a great chance the ice will cause significant damage to the dock and hoist. (The DNR regulations state all docks must be removed by December 15 unless you have a special exemption.) Boats are taken to the boat works for storage or moved onto a trailer and stored. Hoists are lifted and usually left on the bank of the property owner. (In some cases there isn't room, or the owner simply doesn't want to look at the barren hoist, then they are remotely stored.) The dock crews mark the posts (making it easier to install in the spring), take the docks apart, and stack all the lumber on the banks or shore platforms.

Fishing is one of the biggest activities in the autumn.

Image courtesy of Okoboji Tourism and Blue Water Ventures, David Thoreson.

With the cooler weather, bicycling is especially popular on the extensive around-the-lake trail system.

Image courtesy of Okoboji Tourism and Blue Water Ventures, David Thoreson.

WINTER

Winter is long and cold. That pretty much sums it up, but the hardy souls at the lake make the most of it.

The steamships would over-winter in Smith's Bay to protect them from the outgoing ice (circa 1920s).
Image courtesy of Luckybreak/Okoboji.

Fishermen love ice fishing. That is why fish shacks were built, so the fishermen could stay out a long time in relative warmth. If you have never been on the lake when there are 2 to 4 feet of ice beneath you, it is amazing.
Image courtesy of Iowa Great Lakes Maritime Museum.

Ice fishing on Smith's Bay, 2015.
Image courtesy of Fred Cerwick.

It is incredible how easily you can see the fish down in the water when in a darkened fish hut.
Image courtesy of Fred Cerwick.

Images courtesy of Iowa Great Lakes Maritime Museum.

In the past, one source of income was the harvesting of ice for refrigeration. This was also one of the primary reasons the railroads came to the lakes. Crews of men would go out on the lake after the ice was quite thick. Huge blocks were cut and put on a ramp that ran from the lake surface to the awaiting railcars. The ice from Okoboji was considered some of the best available and shipped near and far. Some was kept in a specially built building in Okoboji on the East Lake.

Most people think snowmobiles are relatively new. They have been around since back in the early 1900s. Today, snowmobiles are so popular the Department of Transportation designed the widened highway with a tunnel underneath to allow snowmobiles access from West to East Okoboji.

Images courtesy of Iowa Great Lakes Maritime Museum.

Ice boating used to be a popular activity, and races were held. The boats were made locally, and used not just for sport, but also to get from place to place. Of course you have to watch out for holes in the ice. It's rare to see an ice boat anymore.

Images courtesy of Iowa Great Lakes Maritime Museum.

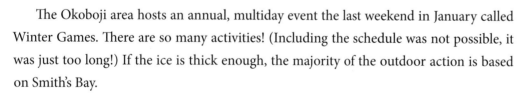

The Okoboji area hosts an annual, multiday event the last weekend in January called Winter Games. There are so many activities! (Including the schedule was not possible, it was just too long!) If the ice is thick enough, the majority of the outdoor action is based on Smith's Bay.

There are events that do not take place outside. The chili competition is always well attended. There is also a pancake feed, chocolate tasting, bridge tournament, and much more. If the snow is good, as many as 20,000 snowmobilers come in for the weekend.

Smith's Bay is typically covered by cars, snowmobiles, and beer tents. Activities include broom hockey, a golf "range" (longest drive), dog sled rides, you name it, during Okoboji's Winter Games.

Image courtesy of Okoboji Tourism and Blue Water Ventures, David Thoreson.

Winter Games Cheerleaders, the Freeze Your Fanny Ride, and the Frozen Fanny Fat Bike Challenge are three of the many facets of the Winter Games.

Images courtesy of Dave Petrick.

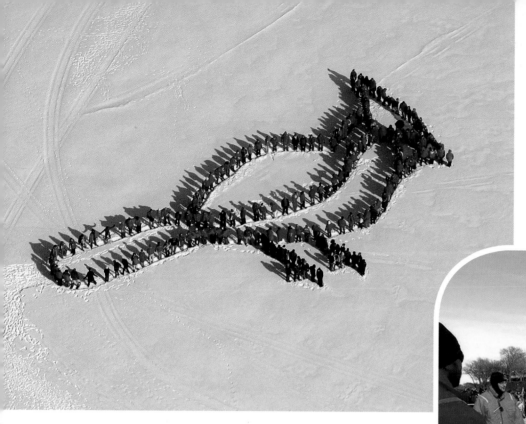

People's Art-on-the-Ice, sponsored by the Friends of Lakeside Lab, always attracts a lot of participants.

Image courtesy of Lakeside Lab.

One of the most popular events, as a spectator, is the Polar Plunge. Participants dress in whatever they want and jump into a newly created hole in the ice. The EMTs are there to help everyone out safely. The best part is that this is a fundraiser.

Image courtesy of Explore Okoboji.

Saturday night is the Burning of the Greens (everyone's dried up Christmas trees) and fireworks over the ice. The sight and sound of the fireworks is incredible—reflecting and booming off the ice.

Image courtesy of Explore Okoboji.

Did you know?

A stripped-down car is put on the ice every winter as a fundraiser for various charities. People bet on the exact time it will fall through the ice. A clock is placed inside and will stop as soon as the car breaks through. The emergency rescue team pulls the car back out as a safety practice exercise.

Images courtesy of Explore Okoboji.

Image courtesy of Jim Hedgpeth.

Even in winter, Okoboji provides beautiful images of nature.

Image courtesy of C. L. Landen II.

Did you know?

Members of the Wilson family have been responsible for documenting the ice in/ice out dates. Gramma Lou Wilson first started keeping track of the dates. Her son, Harry "Zeke" Wilson took over from his mom. Now Zeke's grandson, Kirk Erwin, has taken over the job of traveling around the lakes to confirm that the ice is in or out.

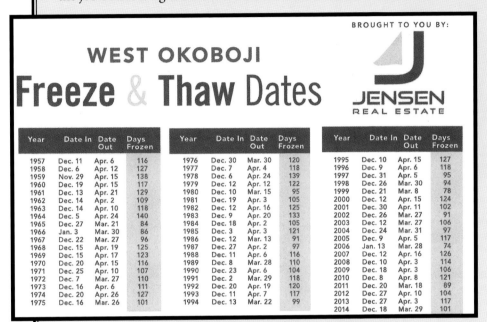

WEST OKOBOJI Freeze & Thaw Dates

Year	Date In	Date Out	Days Frozen	Year	Date In	Date Out	Days Frozen	Year	Date In	Date Out	Days Frozen
1957	Dec. 11	Apr. 6	116	1976	Dec. 30	Mar. 30	120	1995	Dec. 10	Apr. 15	127
1958	Dec. 6	Apr. 12	127	1977	Dec. 7	Apr. 4	118	1996	Dec. 9	Apr. 6	118
1959	Nov. 29	Apr. 15	138	1978	Dec. 6	Apr. 24	139	1997	Dec. 31	Apr. 5	95
1960	Dec. 19	Apr. 15	117	1979	Dec. 12	Apr. 12	122	1998	Dec. 26	Mar. 30	94
1961	Dec. 13	Apr. 21	129	1980	Dec. 10	Mar. 15	95	1999	Dec. 21	Mar. 8	78
1962	Dec. 14	Apr. 2	109	1981	Dec. 19	Apr. 3	105	2000	Dec. 12	Apr. 15	124
1963	Dec. 14	Apr. 10	118	1982	Dec. 12	Apr. 16	125	2001	Dec. 30	Apr. 11	102
1964	Dec. 5	Apr. 24	140	1983	Dec. 9	Apr. 20	133	2002	Dec. 26	Mar. 27	91
1965	Dec. 27	Mar. 21	84	1984	Dec. 18	Apr. 2	105	2003	Dec. 12	Mar. 27	106
1966	Jan. 3	Mar. 30	86	1985	Dec. 3	Apr. 3	121	2004	Dec. 24	Mar. 31	97
1967	Dec. 22	Mar. 27	96	1986	Dec. 12	Mar. 13	91	2005	Dec. 9	Apr. 5	117
1968	Dec. 15	Apr. 19	125	1987	Dec. 27	Apr. 2	97	2006	Jan. 13	Mar. 28	74
1969	Dec. 15	Apr. 17	123	1988	Dec. 11	Apr. 6	116	2007	Dec. 12	Apr. 16	126
1970	Dec. 20	Apr. 15	116	1989	Dec. 8	Mar. 28	110	2008	Dec. 10	Apr. 3	114
1971	Dec. 25	Apr. 10	107	1990	Dec. 23	Apr. 6	104	2009	Dec. 18	Apr. 3	106
1972	Dec. 7	Mar. 27	110	1991	Dec. 2	Mar. 29	118	2010	Dec. 8	Apr. 8	121
1973	Dec. 16	Apr. 6	111	1992	Dec. 20	Apr. 19	120	2011	Dec. 20	Mar. 18	89
1974	Dec. 20	Apr. 26	127	1993	Dec. 11	Apr. 7	117	2012	Dec. 27	Apr. 10	104
1975	Dec. 16	Mar. 26	101	1994	Dec. 13	Mar. 22	99	2013	Dec. 27	Apr. 3	117
								2014	Dec. 18	Mar. 29	101

Image courtesy of Jensen Real Estate.

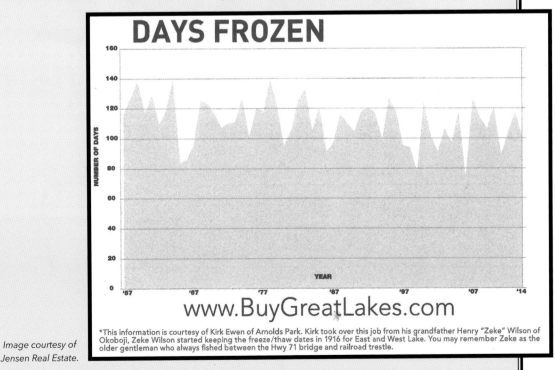

DAYS FROZEN

www.BuyGreatLakes.com

*This information is courtesy of Kirk Ewen of Arnolds Park. Kirk took over this job from his grandfather Henry "Zeke" Wilson of Okoboji. Zeke Wilson started keeping the freeze/thaw dates in 1916 for East and West Lake. You may remember Zeke as the older gentleman who always fished between the Hwy 71 bridge and railroad trestle.

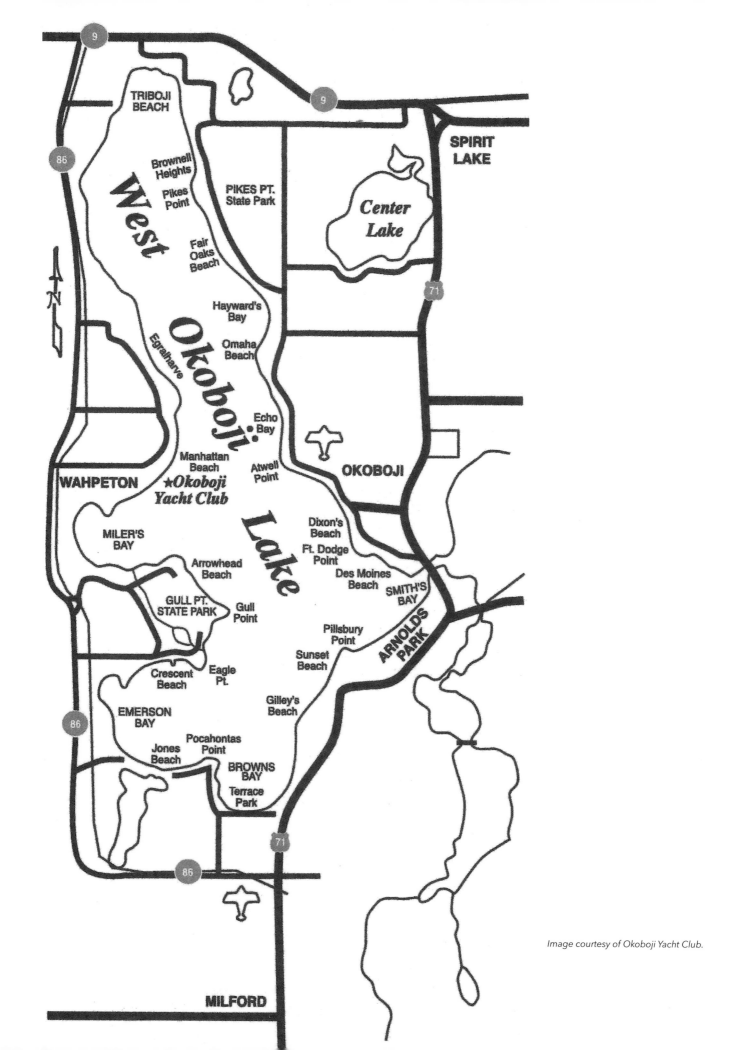

Image courtesy of Okoboji Yacht Club.

8

Lakes, Points, Beaches, and Towns —Where the Names Came From

Dickinson County	The county where Okoboji is located was named for Senator Daniel S. Dickinson of New York in 1857.

LAKES

West Lake Okoboji	Originally called Minnetonka, or "Great Waters" by the Dakota Sioux Indians. Since there was a well-known lake by that name in Minnesota, the lake was renamed West Okoboji.
East Lake Okoboji	Was called Okoboozhy by the Dakota Sioux, which meant "reeds or rushes" and anglicized to Okoboji. As both bodies of water were now called Okoboji, this became East Lake Okoboji.
Spirit Lake	The largest of the lakes was called "Minnie Waukon," which meant Spirit of the Lakes. The French trappers called it "Lac d'Esprit." As the story goes, a canoe piloted by Indians once traveled its waters and never returned. It was haunted. Hence, Spirit Lake.
Upper Gar Lake	Was the farthest north of the original three Gar lakes.
Minnewashta Lake	Originally called Middle Gar. After Abbie Gardner Sharp moved away from the family log cabin on Pillsbury Point, she lived in a small cabin on this lake. Abbie, and her neighbor, Kate Clarke, felt the name "Middle Gar" didn't do this lake justice. They called it "Minnewashta," which was "good or nice" in Dakota Sioux. When that name began to show up on maps, they knew the lake had been renamed.
Lower Gar Lake	There was a proliferation of Gar fish at the base of the three-lake chain. This resulted in the lakes being named Gar.

BAYS, BEACHES, AND POINTS

Smith's Bay	Named for the Smith family. Roderick Smith first came to help bury the victims of the massacre of 1857. He told his family of the beauty of the lakes. Brother Milton arrived and purchased 138.6 acres in 1866, which included all the land from the grade in Okoboji to the road that passes the airport. The family started Smith's Cottages.

Given's Point	Judge Josiah Given had his sons build the first structure here. They were from Des Moines.
Des Moines Beach	The first campers, and later builders, were from Des Moines. Some "residents" included Judge Given, George Dimmit, Charles Breck Dockstader, W. F. Conrad, and Samuel Green.
Fort Dodge Point	Early campers were from Fort Dodge, Iowa. Several prominent citizens then bought lots and built their cottages here.
Dixon Beach	Aaron Dixon purchased property here April 13, 1867. He owned it until August 16, 1882, when he sold it to the railroad. This was first called Maple Grove then Bennett's Beach.
Atwell Point	Named for early resident Mr. R. P. Atwell of Fort Dodge, Iowa.
Echo Bay	If you go out on the water, about halfway from Manhattan Beach, and make noise toward Echo Bay, it will come back to you as an echo.
Omaha Beach/ Point	The first trustee, Artamas Clarke, and campers were from the Omaha area.
Hayward's Bay	William Hayward from Spirit Lake owned this area from about 1894. This was originally called Palmer's Bay.
Fair Oaks Beach	Plenty of oak trees on the land.
Pikes Point	Established in 1892 by Omahans Baum and Patterson. History doesn't tell why it was called Pikes Point.
Brownell Heights	Named for early resident Dr. E. L. Brownell of Spirit Lake.
Triboji	Developed by the Percival family and the *Sioux City Tribune*. Named Triboji for the Tribune and Okoboji.
Raebel's Beach	Owned by Rob Raebel who ran a small resort with his wife.
West Okoboji Harbor	Was created by dredging in 1968.
Van Steenburg Estates	Van Steenburg was a prominent land owner in the area.
Egralharve Beach	G. A. Badgerow of Sioux City named his property for his three sons, Egbert, Ralph, and Harve.
Manhattan Point/ Beach	Owned and developed by D. B. Lyon of Des Moines. After research it is unknown just why it was called Manhattan. Possibly to entice New Yorkers to visit since Prohibition was in force in New York.
Miller's Bay	George B. Miller was one of the first settlers on the west side of the lake.
Arrowhead Beach	Likely named for Indian arrowheads found there.
Gull Point	Named for all the gull birds that regularly were in residence.
Lakewood Park/ Lagoon (now part of Gull Point State Park)	Named by owners J. A. Beck and H. E. Mills. This was dredged in 1911 and was supposed to be a new American Venice.

Eagle Point	American eagles once had a nest in the large tree on this point.
Crescent Beach	Named for the shape of the beach.
Emerson Bay	Named after Samuel and/or T. Emerson who were some of the first settlers in Lakeville township.
Jones Beach	Named for W. H. Jones.
Pocahontas Point	Purchased by Mr. Bruce of Pocahontas County, an attorney for the Rock Island Railroad. The railroad abandoned the project, however others from Pocahontas came into ownership.
Brown's Bay	Named for John M. Brown, homesteader.
Terrace Park	Purchased jointly by Dr. Green and Father McGrath. They then contacted two landscape architects to design what was then a sandy beach. It was laid out, "terraced," and Dr. Green planted 6,000 trees.
Maywood Beach	Named for J. F. May in 1920.
Gilley's Beach	There was a colony of people from Carroll County, including William Gilley. He purchased the property in 1894 and laid it out in lots.
Sunset Beach	Best view of sunsets from this location.
Pillsbury Point	Named for Rev. Samuel Pillsbury of Spirit Lake.

TOWNS

Okoboji	Named for the lake Okoboozhy/Okoboji. Incorporated in 1922 when Arnold's Park threatened annexation.
Spirit Lake	Town named after the lake—Minnie Waukon/Lac d'Esprit/Spirit Lake.
Wahpeton	Named for the Indian chief whose sons helped "purchase" Mrs. Marble from Chief Inkpaduta. The word also means "village or people dwelling in the leaves."
West Okoboji	Formed in 1925–it's just the west end of Lake Okoboji.
Arnold's Park (later Arnolds Park)	In 1882 Miss Hattie Arnold and Miss Ada Shaw were resting in hammocks on the W. B. Arnold property and said, "It is so lovely here, it should have a name. It's as lovely as a park. That's it–Arnold's Park!"

Image courtesy of Iowa Friends of Lakeside Lab.

When people work together, wonderful things happen.

9

PAY IT FORWARD

Private individuals have been of great importance to this amazing lake called West Okoboji. If someone saw a need, he or she found a way to address that need. When people sat down around a table and dreamed, amazing things happened.

Profits from this book are going to the Okoboji Foundation to continue to aid the various organizations that make the Iowa Great Lakes what they are. If you wish to help, listed here are several of the primary organizations and ways to donate your time or treasure.

The best thing a private citizen can do is join a lake association. —John Wills, Okoboji Protective Association President

OKOBOJI FOUNDATION

The Okoboji Foundation's website shows images of stones with the foundation's name. Alongside is the statement, "Okoboji Foundation Logo Stones symbolize the Center Point of Community Giving to Send Ripples of Good throughout the Iowa Great Lakes Region."

According to the Okoboji Foundation's executive director, Mary Freiborg, "The Okoboji Foundation is the community foundation for the Iowa Great Lakes region. As the center point of community giving for vital capital projects, we provide the flexibility to start something new or sustain our region's most treasured facilities and amenities."

Since 1988, the Okoboji Foundation has addressed vital community needs with $2.8 million in grants to a wide variety of nonprofit capital projects. Grants focus on structures, physical property, or equipment to make a lasting, positive impact in the lakes community.

The Okoboji Foundation *Family of Funds* is the local connection for Donor Advised, Nonprofit and Designated Funds. As an affiliate of the Community Foundation of Greater Des Moines, the Okoboji Foundation is also able to offer the Endow Iowa Tax Credit.

The *Okoboji Foundation Legacy Society* acknowledges those who include the foundation in their wills or estate plans. An annual summer Legacy Society Reception is held to say thank you and bring people together who share this ultimate act of giving beyond their lifetime.

For more information, contact Okoboji Foundation: (712) 332-7177, email info@okobojifoundation.org, website www.okobojifoundation.org.

OKOBOJI PROTECTIVE ASSOCIATION

The Okoboji Protective Association (OPA) has a deep history at the lakes. Greg Drees, past president, submitted the following:

At the turn of the twentieth century, when the first cottages were springing up on the shores of West Lake Okoboji, there was born an organization that would protect those early homesteads, a group of notoriety that would evolve later into a renowned environmental watchdog.

In August 1905, the Okoboji Protective Association (OPA) debuted with the objective of protecting the cottages of its members from vandalism, offering a "$100 reward for the detection and arrest of any person feloniously breaking into a cottage or destroying property of any association member and to further the propagation of fish and game through better law enforcement."

The OPA flourished early on, setting its sights less on property protection and more and more on environmental, ecological, and conservation issues. The organization began publishing a remarkable yearly bulletin, the contents of which were diverse, and the collection of which today is a treasured archive.

The voluminous annual editions—which often ran as long as 200 pages, and which were lovingly leather-bound for several years—featured messages from the OPA president, editorials on conservation issues, biographies and obituaries of members, Native American lore and legend, dissertations on the mammal, fish, wildlife, and plant life of the Iowa Great Lakes, and observations of nature and poetry, both good and bad. Perusing each of these bulletins, which were published into the 1940s, is like stepping into a history book.

A chronology of the OPA in its early years can help shape its history and segue into the modern organization's mission to preserve and enhance the water quality and ecological health of West Lake Okoboji and the entire watershed of the Iowa Great Lakes.

- **1906** – The OPA fortuitously recommended to the Iowa legislature that an annual $1 hunting and fishing license be created, with the revenue going to the State Fish and Game Fund to be used to build and maintain fish hatcheries and to finance conservation law enforcement. The OPA had grown to 175 members.

- **1907** – The OPA's Articles of Incorporation were adopted and the group began discussing its first water safety recommendations, including the recommendation that all boat operators wear a life jacket.

- **1910** – The OPA-proposed hunting and fishing license was initiated, netting $100,000 for the Iowa Game and Fish Commission.

- **1912** – A directory of summer cottages on West Lake Okoboji listing the owners' names was published by the OPA.

- **1915** – Illustrating an early interest in providing public access, the OPA encouraged the state Legislature to create state parks on West Lake Okoboji and, also showing its interest in the overall health of the Iowa Great Lakes, donated funds for the construction of a fish hatchery on property between Big Spirit and East Lake Okoboji.

- **1923** – An ode to West Lake Okoboji by OPA member D. A. McBurney opined: "The birds sing nowhere quite so sweet, and nowhere hearts so lightly beat, for heaven and earth both seem to meet around Lake Okoboji."

- **1926** – Due in large part to effective lobbying by the OPA, more fish and game regulations were passed by the Iowa Game and Fish Commission.

- **1927** – An editorial in the OPA bulletin by President John M. Guild referred to the spring migration of songbirds back into the lakes area. He urged residents to "keep the thick, luxuriant vegetation on lakeside banks. The birds love it, the habitat serves as blessed bird sanctuaries."

- **1930** – In a speech to the OPA, Iowa Senator Leslie Francis said, "My friends, we have in this community the most valuable single asset in the state of Iowa—West Lake Okoboji." OPA membership dues swell to $2 per year.

- **1940** – Spearheaded by the OPA, the Iowa Lakes Sewage Diversion System, later to be known as the IGL Sanitary Sewer District, is under construction.

Over the more than seventy years hence, the OPA has worked tirelessly for the protection of West Lake Okoboji and the Iowa Great Lakes watershed, and its partnerships and accomplishments have proven to be deep and successful. The OPA took the lead in the first Iowa Great Lakes watershed study, was a founding member of the Dickinson County Clean Water Alliance (CWA), helped found Friends of Lakeside Lab in providing student scholarships at Iowa Lakeside Lab and raising public awareness of water quality issues, and has been an active partner with the Department of Natural Resources (DNR) in prolific wetland restoration projects in the lakes area.

Today the OPA is strongly involved with water quality and water safety issues. Partnering with CWA and the DNR, the OPA helps fund and encourages the use of Low Impact Development techniques in area development and construction projects, utilizing rain gardens, wetland basins and bioswales to manage storm-water runoff.

Through education and funding, the OPA has raised awareness of the threat of aquatic invasive species into the Iowa Great Lakes chain and was a large player in the construction of an electric fish barrier at the Lower Gar outlet to prevent the infestation of Asian carp into the system.

The OPA has worked closely with the Iowa Great Lakes Water Safety Council and the DNR to improve water safety. With OPA influence, a nighttime boating speed limit was established, the alcohol level limit for boaters was lowered to match the .08 level of motorized vehicle operators, a new boat noise ordinance was enacted, and the DNR Lake Patrol staff and boat fleet have been greatly strengthened.

The nonprofit OPA is governed by a board of directors and is comprised of dues-paying members who are passionate about not only the preservation and enhancement of West Lake Okoboji but of the entire Iowa Great Lakes watershed and the ecological and conservation health of the lakes communities. Won't you join us in this mission?

For more information on the Okoboji Protective Association, go to
www.okobojiprotectiveassociation.org.

FRIENDS OF LAKESIDE LAB

Supporting the Iowa Lakeside Laboratory as a community resource for environmental education, water quality monitoring, and research is the mission of the Friends of Lakeside Lab.

A crisis was at hand in December 1991. It looked like the end of the Lakeside Lab due to funding restraints and other factors. Once again the locals came to the help of one of the best assets of the lake. Community members formed a Lakeside Task Force, and with the

guidance of the University of Okoboji Foundation (today the Okoboji Foundation), the incredible assets of the lab, and its opportunities for expansion, were discussed.

The Lakeside Task Force findings determined there was abundant community support for Lakeside to proceed with a plan to sustain and grow its future. As Lakeside is a Board of Regents institution, they contacted the Iowa Board of Regents and university presidents to set up a meeting. Negotiating with the VIPs did not come easily, according to Sue Richter, a key player in the Task Force, so they hatched a plan to invite them to tour Lakeside and take them on a boat ride. It was one of those beautiful Okoboji days.

"We boarded the boat and cruised into the middle of West Okoboji," recalls Richter with a mischievous sparkle in her eyes, "and then we turned the boat motor off. Silence. They had to listen to what we had to say."

The Regents had requested the community take greater financial responsibility in lab operations, but the community demanded more in return: expanded, year-round environmental education opportunities for learners of all ages, and the sharing of university expertise to protect the valuable water quality resources of the Iowa Great Lakes through water quality monitoring and research.

In response, the Iowa Board of Regents formed an eight-point plan in 1993 and tasked the Okoboji community with increasing financial support for Lakeside operations and expanding community programs and liaison. The same year, the community members who had advocated for Lakeside formed the Friends of Lakeside Lab, and by 1996 had incorporated as a tax-exempt, nonprofit organization with the mission to "support Iowa Lakeside Laboratory as a community resource for environmental education, water quality monitoring, and research."

A pleased Sue Richter, "They heard us!"

Upon incorporation, the Friends organization's first task was to create the infrastructure for their mission. Traditionally a summer operation, Lakeside lacked winterized facilities to support year-round programming and research. The Friends began a campaign to raise funds to build Lakeside's first year-round facility, the Waitt Lab, named after major donors Norman Waitt and Andrea Waitt (today Andrea Waitt Carlton).

Besides the Waitt Lab, the Friends have provided for the expansion of Lakeside education programs to include pre-K through 12th grade and the life-long learners. There are abundant volunteer opportunities and year-round programming. They have also provided increased scholarship and research fellowships for students and have established an endowment to sustain Lakeside's water quality monitoring, education, and research programs.

For more information on the Friends of Lakeside Lab,
go to www.friendsoflakesidelab.org

IOWA GREAT LAKES ASSOCIATION

This is the newest of the organizations and is not a 501(c)(3) charity. For a very good reason! IGLA is the only organization that can hire lobbyists and/or take a case to court. This organization represents the side of the lake residents and provides support for many of the charitable organizations at the lakes.

The IGLA was formed in 2008 to address the possibility of hog confinement structures near the lakes. IGLA worked with other locals and the agricultural community to come up with a solution for all. Most recently, IGLA was involved in getting the electric barrier funded and built to stop invasive fish from entering the Iowa Great Lakes.

Today, IGLA has transitioned into a multi-issue organization that strives to keep all members abreast of current issues and initiatives that may affect the Iowa Great Lakes.

For more information, go to www.iagreatlakes.com.

IOWA GREAT LAKES WATER SAFETY COUNCIL

The Water Safety Council (WSC) was started in 2002 by former DNR Dickinson County head Gary Owen with backing from lakes resident Chuck Long.

The WSC is dedicated to promoting boating and water safety along with improved water quality. One of their first actions was to purchase multichannel portable radios and a multichannel base station at the Gull Point State Park headquarters. Communication has been a strong focus for this group. They have also been instrumental in beefing up the Lake Patrol fleet of boats. Basically, if the subject is safety on the water, the WSC is probably involved. The WSC is strengthening its mission to improve water safety and water quality through cooperation.

For more information, go to www.watersafetycouncil.org.

DICKINSON COUNTY
CLEAN WATER ALLIANCE

United to keep our lakes alive!

DICKINSON COUNTY
CLEAN WATER ALLIANCE

The Clean Water Alliance (CWA) is the messenger of the clean water activities to the people of Dickinson County. It was started by the Iowa Natural Heritage Foundation and the Dickinson Soil and Water Conservation District around 1991 or 1992.

This alliance provides a great resource for member groups. CWA put member partners together to achieve a goal and help with grant writing and so far has worked with eighty-one partners.

The CWA educates the people of Dickinson County and its visitors about clean water issues and associated projects through public seminars and education opportunities. This group has been especially helpful in getting the word out about rain gardens and the need to filter runoff water before it gets into the lake system.

For more information, go to http://cleanwateralliance.net/blog.

DICKINSON COUNTY TRAILS BOARD
AND *FRIENDS OF THE TRAILS*

This is a prime example of what a group of citizens can accomplish when they dream.

In the early 1990s a group of sports-minded individuals gathered around a table with a large map of the county. Their objective was to dream what could be done with unlimited funds. Joani Schneider and Eric Hoien went to the conservation board and asked for start-up money. They got that seed money, and in October 1992 the first part of the trails spine (an extensive system of trails for biking and walking around the lakes) opened. Where they could use the old rail beds, they did. When they couldn't use former railways, they went to the appropriate towns and worked to secure a safe route. (See trail map, page 180.)

In 2015 the main spine was resurfaced and three other trails were completed. In the future they hope to add a trail along the east side of East Okoboji going from Highway 9, along M56 and toward Arnolds Park past Bridges Bay. Another goal is an east/west trail along an abandoned rail line from Spirit Lake toward Superior—and eventually to Sibley.

For more information, go to http://dickinsoncountytrails.com.

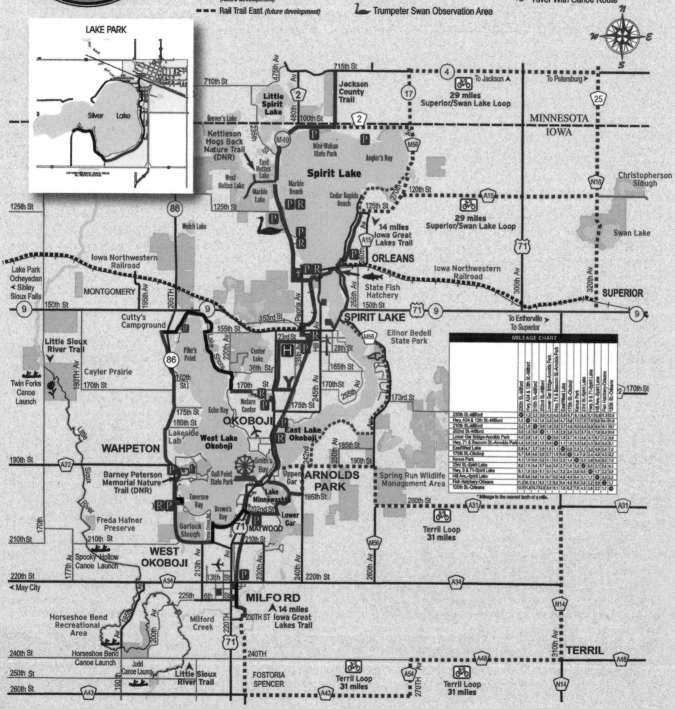

RESOURCES

This book is a compilation from many sources and resources. My family owns several books on the lakes, but I have also borrowed many from the Spirit Lake Public Library, the Iowa Great Lakes Maritime Museum, and many friends. The library has online historical newspaper articles, which have been a huge asset. I appreciate the *Dickinson County News* for authorizing me to use any information and images that have been published over the years in the local papers.

I could never have correctly written the Nature/Ecology chapter without the immense help from Jane Shuttleworth with Lakeside Lab and Mike Hawkins with the Iowa Department of Natural Resources.

So many current photographs are courtesy of David Thoreson. His work is amazing. Thanks also go to photographer Fred Cerwick for providing many images and his help touching up several historic photographs.

There is a great deal more to learn about the massacre, and other past events. I urge you to dig a bit deeper if that interests you. Listed here are the various publications that I have used, followed by the many individuals who have given me their time and stories. This could never have been done without all of you!

125 Year Book Committee. *Arnolds Park Amusement Park*, 2015.

Craig, Brian J. *Postcards from the Lakes*. Milford, Iowa: Brian J. Craig, 2009.

Elston, Hattie P. *White Men Follow After*. Arnolds Park, Iowa: Hattie P. Elston, 1946.

Hedgpeth, Cristy Clarke and Wendy Louis Poston. *The History and Memories of Des Moines Beach*. Omaha, Nebraska: Cristy C. Hedgpeth and Wendy L. Poston, 2003.

Hofsommer, Don. *Prairie Oasis*. Plainview, Texas: Donovan L. Hofsmommer, 1975.

Jensen, Mary. *A Centennial Cruise on the Iowa Great Lakes*. Cedar Falls, Iowa: Mary Jensen, 1976.

LaFoy, R. Aubrey. *Okoboji Remembered and Other Stories*. Aubrey LaFoy.

LaFoy, R. Aubrey. *Down Memory Lane of the Iowa Great Lakes*. Aubrey LaFoy, 1994.

LaFoy, R. Aubrey. *Iowa Great Lakes Revisited*, Aubrey LaFoy, 1995.

LaFoy, R. Aubrey. *Strolling Down Memory Lane at the Iowa Great Lakes*. Aubrey LaFoy, 2014.

Morris, O. M. *Picturesque Souvenir of Spirit and Okoboji Lakes*, 1896.

Parsons, John W. and Stephen Kennedy. *Okoboji Gold*. Okoboji, Iowa: John W. Parsons, 1995.

Smith, Peggy. *Arnolds Park*. Arnolds Park, Iowa: Peggy Schenk Smith, 1976.

Smith, R. A. *A History of Dickinson County Iowa*. R. A. Smith, 1902.

Spirit Lake Library. *Remembering the Iowas Great Lakes (series)*. Spirit Lake, Iowa: Friends of the Spirit Lake Library.

Spirit Lake Library. *The Iowa Great Lakes Remembers: A Look at the Past, A Dream for the Future*. Spirit Lake, Iowa: Friends of the Spirit Lake Library, 2006.

Wright, Mrs. William Frank. *The Lake Region. Blue Book and Club Directory of Spirit Lake and Vicinity*. Mrs. W. F. Wright, 1906.

Wilson, Fred. *The Girl on a Horse*. Spirit Lake, Iowa: Fred Wilson, 1990.

Magazines: *Okoboji Magazine, Vacation Okoboji*.

Websites: Explore Okoboji, Luckybreak/Okoboji.

ACKNOWLEDGMENTS

And a special thanks to these incredible people who shared family scrapbooks, provided photographs, and told the stories that filled this book.

Steve Anderson	Iowa Great Lakes Sanitary District
Libby Diers Anderson	
Julie Andres	Mau Marine
Durinda Aspleaf	Emporium
Dick Baker	University of Iowa
Thomas Bellaire	
Art Bettis	University of Iowa
John Brown	The New Inn & Central Bank
Lesleigh Buck	
Paula Buenger	*Dickinson County News*
Jim Carpenter	Milford Fire Chief
Josh Carr	Camp Foster
Fred Cerwick	Photographer
Steve Christensen	
Brian Craig	
Dennis Daly	Okoboji City Manager
Cynthia Davis	Spirit Lake Library
Patty Davis	
Greg Drees	
Beth Ehler	Lakeshore Center at Okoboji (Presbyterian)
Bob and Mary Ellen Evans	
Rob Eves	
Kelli Fararr	
Brad Fararr	
Julie Fillenwarth	Fillenwarth's Beach Resort
Mary Ross Franken	

Mary Fryberg	Okoboji Foundation
Theresa Garvey	
Larry Goodwin	The New Inn
Colleen Graham	
Martha Green	
Boots Gross	Dickinson Country Auditor's office
Kenny Halibur	Halibur Docks
Mike Hawkins	Iowa Department of Natural Resources
Jim Hedgpeth	
Helen Hewitt	
Mike Hoeppner	Village West
Eric Hoien	
Doyne Wilson Hummel	
Jim and Michael Jensen	Jensen Real Estate
Trevor Johnson	KUOO
Bryan Johnson	Lake Okoboji United Methodist Camp
Doug Kading	Camp Okoboji
Dakota Keller	Lakeside Lab
Mary Kennedy	Iowa Great Lakes Maritime Museum
Keith Kennedy	
Kevin Kooima	Kooima Lakes Service
Aubrey LaFoy	
Mary, Patty & C. L. Landen	
Mike Lannoo	Lakeside Lab
Anitra Wolf Larson	IGLA
Denny Linn	Okoboji Classic Cars Museum
Loraine Wilson Little	
Sharon London	
Chuck Long	Manhattan Beach
Bill Maas	
Jean Martin	Dickinson County Trails Board
Don McCulloch	
Bruce McWilliams	Lakeside Lab
Walt & Barb Mendenhall	
Chuck Montange	Manhattan Beach

Rikki Norton	Crescent Beach Lodge
Russ Oechslin	Photographer
Okoboji Classic Cars Museum	
Okoboji Yacht Club	
Don Oleson	
Lisa Pelto and team	Concierge Marketing
Phil Peterson	Water Safety Council
Dave Petrick	Photographer
Jesse Randall	ISU Forestry
TJ Reardon	
Herman Richter	The Three Sons
Molly Rohlfsen	Okoboji Tourism
Carl Ross	
Kathy Ross Saunders	
Joani Schneider	
Cindy Schubert	Dickinson County Historical Museum
Susan Everist Scott	
Jane Shuttleworth	Lakeside Lab
Bruce and Vicky Smith	
Allen Smith	
Craig Smith	
Leslie Suhr	
David Thoreson	Blue Water Ventures
Tom Tourville	Midwest Publications
Bob Trader	
Myrna Wagner	*Okoboji Magazine*
Doris Welle	*Dickinson County News*
Sandra Wendel	Editor
John Wills	Clean Water Alliance & Water Quality Commission
Craig Wilson	Certified arborist
Carina Woodward	Okoboji Tourism

INDEX

About the Author

Cristy (Cris) Clarke Hedgpeth has lived most of her life between Omaha, Nebraska, and Okoboji, Iowa.

Cris graduated with a BFA from Colorado State University in 1975. She worked as a commercial interior designer until the birth of her second daughter in 1990. Her mother, Sally Searle Clarke, always told her, "Your community gives to you, you need to give back to your community." Cris has been involved with several charitable organizations.

Although not a true writer, Cris has written five cookbooks. They were done so she, and her family and friends, had a place to turn for special recipes. (If you had to describe Cris in one word, it would be organized.) In 2003, Cris, and good friend Wendy Louis Poston, wrote *The History and Memories of Des Moines Beach*—about their area of West Lake Okoboji. The two women realized how much history was being lost after both of their mothers had recently passed away.

Cris is passionate about history, and is concerned by the loss of it. If she has one "pearl of wisdom" she shares with just about anyone she meets, it is to take oral histories. Sit down with the older generation and ask questions like, "What was it like when…" Record their answers. You will never regret it, and when they are no longer around, you will wish you had asked those questions, she advises.

In preparation for their move from Omaha to North Carolina, she has resigned from most of the boards she served on. But what to do with her time? *OKOBOJI: Over 160 Years of History and Images* was the result.

Cris, and her husband, Jim, now split their time between Okoboji and Brevard, North Carolina. Their family include daughters and sons-in-law Alex and Dave Esarey and Kate and Drew Helm, and granddaughter Lyla Helm.

Cristy Clarke Hedgpeth